THE CHRISTOPHER PARKENING GUITAR METHOD, VOL. 2

THE ART AND TECHNIQUE OF THE CLASSICAL GUITAR

In Collabobration with David Brandon

The drawings in Figures 21, 22, and 26 are © 1994 and 1995 by Kris Ellingsen.
Used by Permission.

The following pieces are © 1997 by David Brandon and have been used by
permission: Spanish Ballad, Mazurka, Toccata, Canción, Interlude,
French Lullaby, Prelude in E Minor, all exercises except #7, Twenty-Minute Workout,
and arrangements of Silent Night, Russian Folk Song, Tarantella,
Carol of the Bells, Scarborough Fair, and Catalonian Folk Song.

ISBN 978-0-7935-8521-2

7777 W. BLUEMOUND RD. P.O. BOX 13819 MILWAUKEE, WI 53213

Visit Hal Leonard Online at
www.halleonard.com

Acknowledgements

My special thanks to the following talented individuals who contributed much insight and numerous valuable suggestions: Muriel Anderson, Scott Bach, Jim Fagen, Scott and Amy Faris, Michael Kurtz, John Nelson, Wayne Peabody, Patrick Russ, John Sutherland, David Thomas, David Thompson, Mark and Kathy Tyers, and Paul Wilson. Also thanks to the many students who have offered help along the way.

Material for the sections on Success vs. Excellence and Self-discipline is based on two sermons by John MacArthur, Jr., my faithful pastor and friend.

My gratitude also goes to Jim Fagen for his painstaking job of proofreading the music.

Illustrations were provided by the gifted Kris Ellingsen.

My deep appreciation goes to Terry Duggan for the photographs in this book.

I would also like to thank my friend and collaborator, David Brandon, who prepared and edited the initial text and contributed many original compositions and arrangements to this book.

Text and music layout was produced by David Brandon using exclusively *Finale* and *WordPerfect* for the Macintosh. Thanks to Randy Koonce and Lanny Fiel for technical advice.

Dedication

To my wife Theresa,
my father, mother and sister,
for their untiring, loving guidance
and devotion to my music.

—Christopher Parkening

In loving memory of my mom,
whose great encouragement supported me
in my writing and in my music.

—David Brandon

The Christopher Parkening Discography

In the Spanish Style CDC-7-47194-2

Parkening Plays Bach CDC-7-47191-2

Simple Gifts CDC-7-47525-2

A Bach Celebration CDC-7-47195-2

Pleasures of Their Company CDC-7-47196-2

Virtuoso Duets CDC-7-49406-2

A Tribute to Segovia CDC-7-49404-2

Joaquin Rodrigo and William Walton Concertos CDC-7-54665-2

The Artistry of Christopher Parkening CDC-7-54853-2-5

Christopher Parkening – The Great Recordings ZDCB-54905-2-7

Parkening Plays Vivaldi CDC-5-55052-2

*Angels' Glory SK 62723

*All albums distributed by EMI/Angel Records except *Angels' Glory*,
distributed by Sony Classical.

Contents

Performing in Boston
Courtesy Worcester Telegram & Gazette

Introduction

The second volume of *The Christopher Parkening Guitar Method* is based on the same premise as the first: to learn guitar technique and musicianship by playing beautiful pieces of music. Practicing is more enjoyable and rewarding while working on exciting and inspiring compositions instead of dry exercises.

This present volume is divided into two main sections. Part One deals with learning notes in upper positions (Volume One covers only the first position) and introduces many new techniques. Part Two consists of repertoire that enables the student to develop technique and musicianship more fully. This section is arranged by period or style, rather than by difficulty. Thus, the student is able to choose his own music and gain a perspective on guitar literature as a whole. Also, what is easy for one student may be difficult for another, so grading pieces at this level is nearly impossible. In fact, the student may wish to attempt pieces from the repertoire section of this book while still studying from the technique section. Use this book flexibly, modifying it to meet your own individual needs.

It is important to keep musicality as the final goal, with technique only a means to an end. Strive for a beautiful sound on each piece. Fully explore the nuances of style and interpretation, which I will later cover in detail.

Above all, strive for personal excellence. True success is not measured by worldly accomplishment or by comparison with others. Rather, it is working with diligence, to the best of your ability, toward achieving excellence in whatever task you have set before you.

Performing at the White House

Part I

Technique

Notes on the First String*

Observe that the notes ascend alphabetically in whole-steps, except for the half-steps between E and F and between B and C. This pattern is consistent on every string, so by knowing just one note on any string you will be able to find the others. In the practice scale, the left-hand fingering is divided into three main areas: low, medium, and high. Keep your 1st finger of the left hand resting lightly on the string when shifting positions. This makes the shift more secure. Concentrate on the names of notes as well as finger placement.

Memorize: **Practice Scale #1**

E F G A B C D E

Fret: 0 1 3 5 7 8 10 12

The left-hand *position* is determined by the fret where the index finger falls. For instance, in 7th position the 1st finger will play notes on the 7th fret and the 2nd finger will play notes on the 8th fret, etc. These scales and exercises were created primarily for the purpose of learning the notes on the neck. It is rare to finger a whole passage on the same string as notated here.

Exercise #1

Exercise #2 (Bach)

The high F in this exercise is played on the 13th fret. The notes start over at the 12th fret with E (an octave higher than the open E).

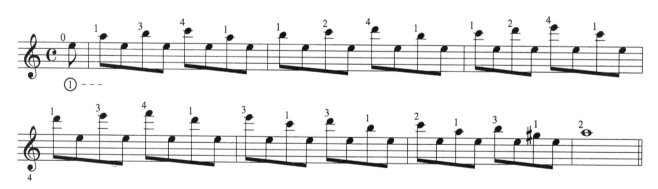

---

*This guitar method teaches upper position note reading one string at a time. First, the student learns all the natural notes on the first string to the 12th fret. Next, we add all the natural notes on the 2nd string, often relating these notes to the first string. When fingering guitar music, the highest note dictates where the rest of the chord (or passage) will be played. For instance, if a 1st string high B is required, the student would have to find other notes in the passage in relation to the B. This approach will become obvious as you proceed through the book.

Guide and Pivot Fingers

Two important principles will facilitate left-hand fingering: the *pivot* finger and the *guide* finger. A pivot is a finger that stays in place as an anchor while other fingers move around it. A guide is one that stays on a string when shifting to another position and is sometimes notated with a dash before the finger number on the note in the new position. It is important to release the pressure slightly to avoid a sliding sound. Apply these two principles whenever possible to maximize left-hand accuracy.

SPANISH BALLAD

Try rest stroke on the first melody note of each measure for greater clarity and balance. Use guide fingers whenever possible.

Practice Tip:
    Practicing correctly is vital to your development as a guitarist. Some players prefer rigid routines and others favor more flexibility. Generally speaking, your practice sessions could be divided to include work in these areas:

Technique	10 minutes to one hour
New repertoire	30 minutes to two hours
Old repertoire	20 minutes to two hours
Sightreading	As needed
Theory	As needed

    During the course of your study you will find there are certain technical issues every guitarist must address. If you cannot find a piece or need more work involving a certain technical aspect, you should supplement your practice with exercises. As you progress, you might spend less time on technique and more time on repertoire. Many guitarists prefer to schedule a certain time of day to practice. Decide on what works best for you personally. More important than the amount of time spent, however, is to set specific goals so you can measure the results of your practice.

Vibrato

The technique of vibrato involves wavering the pitch of a note for shading or expressive purposes. It can add great emotional intensity to a passage and is also effective in achieving proper intonation (playing in tune). *Horizontal* vibrato is achieved by holding a note firmly and moving the left arm from the elbow rapidly back and forth parallel to the neck. The finger stays in place on the string, and the elbow remains stationary. This pushing and pulling motion forces the string to slide back and forth across the fret, causing the note to go sharp and flat. This can also be done without the thumb touching the back of the neck.

Vertical vibrato (fig. 1) is achieved by bending the string up and down parallel to the fret. The movement is done solely by the finger from the second joint. This type of vibrato is often used in the first position where the horizontal motion is not as effective, but it only allows for raising the note. The pitch cannot be lowered in this manner.

It is important to develop the ability to control both the width and speed of the vibrato. A helpful exercise is to put the 2nd finger on the 2nd string at the 10th fret, set your metronome at a moderate speed (try 60), and practice vibrato at four fluctuations per click. You can use the sound of the side of your left hand hitting against the guitar to help you keep beat. Experiment on different strings with each finger and vary the tempo settings to increase your mastery of this vital technique.

Fig. 1 Vertical vibrato on second string.

Try using vibrato on the following two melody lines:

Exercise #3 (Picardy)

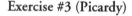

Exercise #4 (Holst)

Dotted Eighth Notes

The following piece contains a prominent rhythmic figure:

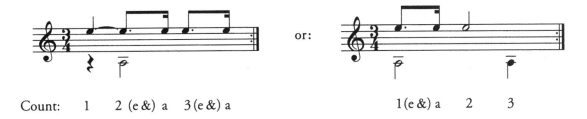

Count: 1 (e &) a

In learning a difficult rhythm, it is sometimes helpful to tap it out or play it on open strings as follows:

or:

Count: 1   2 (e &) a   3 (e &) a   1 (e &) a   2   3

MAZURKA

Set the thumb on the previously played bass note at each rest. This will stop (*dampen*) the string from ringing, achieving clarity in the bass line.

13

Quality of Sound

There are two elusive qualities that separate *guitarists* from ordinary guitar players: a beautiful sound and the ability to play legato. Technical details regarding sound production and nail filing are found in Appendix A at the end of the book. It would be beneficial to study that section now and refer to it again throughout your study. Strive for a pure, full rich tone without the extra noise of fingernail clicks, left-hand squeaks, etc. Play with sufficient volume in order to develop a wide dynamic range. Develop a variety of tonal colors as you strive for a beautiful sound.

To play legato, each note should be connected to the next without a perceptible break. The fingers of both hands should work in unison with extremely quick changes between notes. This movement is similar to the way a mime works: you see one position and then the next, but not the motion in between. It is certainly one of the most difficult qualities to achieve on the guitar, but well worth the effort.

Practice Tip:

One element of proper practicing is problem solving. You will encounter some obstacles in taking a piece from sightreading to a polished performance. Here is a three-step process for overcoming these hurdles:

1) Observe 2) Analyze 3) Correct

In other words, define the problem, analyze how it can be overcome, and implement the solution by correct repetition. By breaking down pieces in this manner and putting them back together again, you will have learned a secret to effective practicing.

SILENT NIGHT

F. Gruber

Strive for a legato melody with a beautiful sound Use vibrato on high notes. Dampen bass notes with the thumb on each rest, especially when changing bass notes. The rests between bass notes of the same pitch need not be taken literally.

Slur Technique

The *slur* (also called *ligado*) is a technique in which you pluck one note and then sound a second note with a left-hand finger only. It is notated with a curved line between two notes of different pitch. This looks the same as a tie, but a tie connects two notes of the same pitch.

To execute an ascending slur, or *hammer-on*, bring the left-hand fingertip down on the string with sufficient force to sound a second note after plucking the first. If the first note is a fretted one, leave that finger in place when the second note is hammered-on.

In a descending slur, or *pull-off*, the left-hand finger actually "plucks" the string as it is taken off (see photos). The finger pulls downward and into the next higher string, as in a "rest stroke" for the right hand (unless, of course, it is already on the first string). If you want the adjacent string to ring, use a "free stroke" slur, where you miss the next higher string with your pull-off finger instead of plucking into it. If both notes are fretted, it is important to have both fingers in place on the string before the pull-off occurs. On all slurs, keep the left hand parallel to the fingerboard, stay close to the fret (not in the center between the frets), and play on the center of the fingertip.

Fig. 2 Preparation of a descending slur.

Fig. 3 Release of descending slur into the next string.

Try the following exercises on different strings to familiarize yourself with the slur technique. Leave the fingers on as you ascend in hammer-ons.

Exercise #5

Exercise #6

*This slur is pictured in the above photos.

The next slur study is one of my personal favorites. If practiced correctly, it will build accuracy, dexterity and left-hand strength. This exercise is for the left hand only and can be practiced up and down the neck. In moving up the neck at the end of the second beat, the 1st finger slides from F to F#, thus starting a new position. In the descending exercise, the 4th finger slides down a half-step, thereby changing positions one fret lower. This is notated by a straight line between the notes. When sliding, keep sufficient pressure on the string to sound the second note. For more work on slurs, I recommend Segovia's *Slur Exercises* (Columbia Music Co.) and the more advanced *Study #11* (Op. 6, no. 3) by Fernando Sor.

Practice Tip:

When using slurs, concentrate on achieving evenness in both the volume and duration of each note. To help equalize the difference in sound between hammer-ons and pull-offs, the hammer-on will need a little extra force. Be sure not to hammer-on or pull-off too quickly, but give each note equal value.

Exercise #7a

Exercise #7b

TOCCATA

Use light, even pull-offs to the open E string. Sometimes it is necessary to lightly file the left-hand calluses to avoid a raspy pull-off sound. For more left-hand security, try riding along the neck with the underside of the hand, just opposite the 1st finger knuckle.

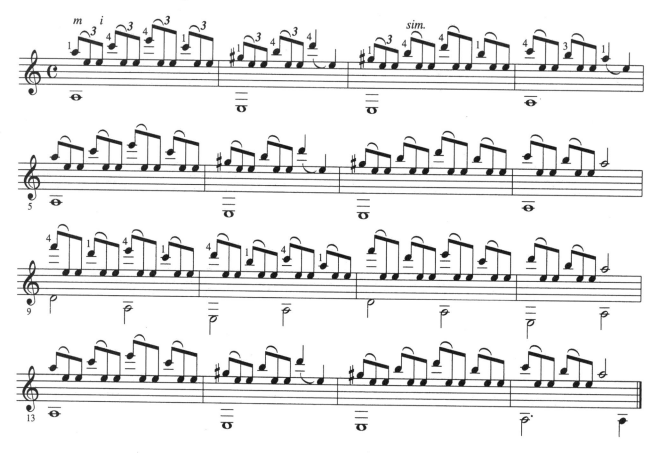

16

Grace Notes

Grace notes are ornaments that add variation and color to a passage of music. They are notated as small slurred notes that appear before a normal size note. In the following examples, the first grace note is played simultaneously with the bass note on the beat. The time value of the grace note is not counted in the rhythm of the bar and must be subtracted from that of the adjacent note.

A more in depth discussion of ornamentation appears on page 54.

Two Baroque Dances

The next two pieces help demonstrate the slur technique and were written for the Baroque guitar in Italy (1646). This instrument had five sets of double strings called *courses*.

CANARIO

CARLO CALVI

This piece is played in 2nd position, i.e., the 1st finger operates on the 2nd fret, the 2nd finger on the 3rd, etc.

DANZA

Carlo Calvi

More Work in 2nd Position

The following two studies are excellent technique builders written in 2nd position. Because they contain no open strings they can be played in any position on the neck. Remember that open string notes can be found on the next lower string as the diagram illustrates:

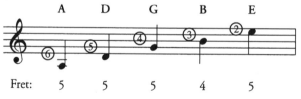

Exercise #8

Exercise #9

Repeat Terms and Signs

D.C. al Fine	Return to the beginning and play to the *Fine*.
D.S. al Fine	Return to the 𝄋 and play to the *Fine*.
D.C. al Coda	Return to the beginning, play to the ⊕ and skip to the *Coda*.
D.S. al Coda	Return to the 𝄋, play to the ⊕ and skip to the *Coda*.

SPANISH WALTZ

ANONYMOUS

For extra practice on the slurred passages in mm. 1 and 5, try using 3rd and 4th fingers.

D.C. al Fine

19

Notes on the Second String

Memorize:

Practice Scale #2

Fret: 0   1   3   5   6   8   10   12

Exercise #10 Notice the key signature change: F on the 6th fret now moves to F# on the 7th fret.

Exercise #11 (Smetana)

Exercise #12 (Grieg)

Practice Tip:

As you practice, periodically ask yourself questions regarding the quality of your progress. Here are a few examples:

- Are you sitting correctly, with a proper balance between security and relaxation?
- Are your hands positioned correctly—with knuckles roughly parallel to the strings?
- Are your nails filed smoothly and correctly so there is no catching or clicking on the strings?
- Is your guitar properly in tune?
- Are you playing the notes and rhythmic values accurately?
- Are your slurs even in volume and rhythm?
- Are you playing legato and with a beautiful sound?
- Are you playing cleanly without excessive noise or mistakes?
- Are you playing musically?

Harmonics
(Natural)

A *harmonic* is a chime-like overtone produced when you lightly touch a string at certain points with a finger while plucking it with another. These points, called *nodes*, are found by dividing the string length in half, 3rds, 4ths, 5ths, etc. You must touch the string directly over the metal fret (without depressing it) and remove your finger as soon as you have plucked the note. (fig. 4) This will result in a harmonic. These work best at frets 12, 7 (or 19), and 5, as the chart indicates. You will also find them at 9 (same as 4 or 16). *Artificial harmonics* will be discussed later.

Unfortunately, there is much discrepancy found in guitar literature regarding the notation of harmonics. They are generally written as diamond shaped notes indicating the actual sounding pitch. Occasionally they will be written an octave lower than they sound. In rare cases, they may reflect the pitch of the natural note at that location, not the harmonic. Sometimes they have an "o" written above or below the note.

Fig. 4 Natural harmonic on the 7th fret.

Here are four examples of the notation. The first two show how natural harmonics are written in this book. They indicate the actual sounding pitch. The other two are less commonly used, but all four represent the same pitch.

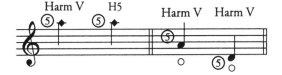

The following table shows the most common natural harmonics. Notice that some are identical in pitch. For example: 6th string, 5th fret equals 5th string, 7th fret. You can tune the guitar by matching these harmonics in unison. (See page 50.)

Table of Natural Harmonics

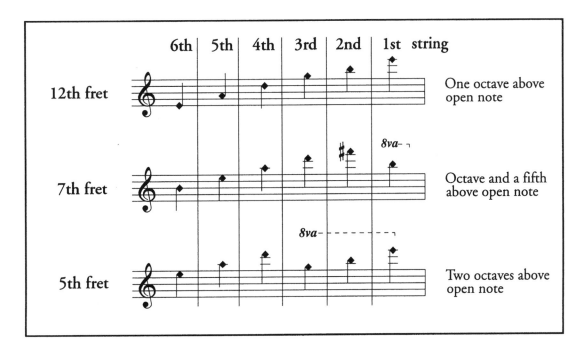

Harmonics (cont.)

Exercise #13

Natural Harmonics...

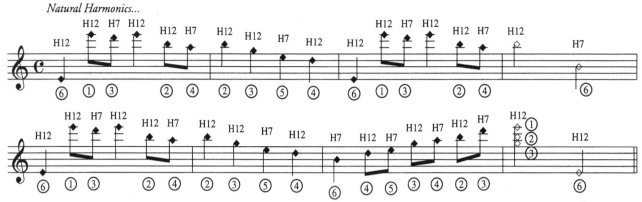

This next piece uses notes on the 2nd string in relation to the 1st string. Remember that generally the highest note of a chord dictates where the other notes in the chord or passage should be played. Always use the most convenient fingering unless musical interpretation dictates an alternate.

Canción is based on the interval of a third (in the first chord, G and B are three notes apart). It is helpful to leave the left-hand first finger on the string as a guide when descending on the 3rds. The open B after each third is called a *pedal tone*—a stationary note around which other voices move. Be sure to let the highest note ring while playing the pedal tone. Strive for a legato sound on all transitions.

CANCIÓN

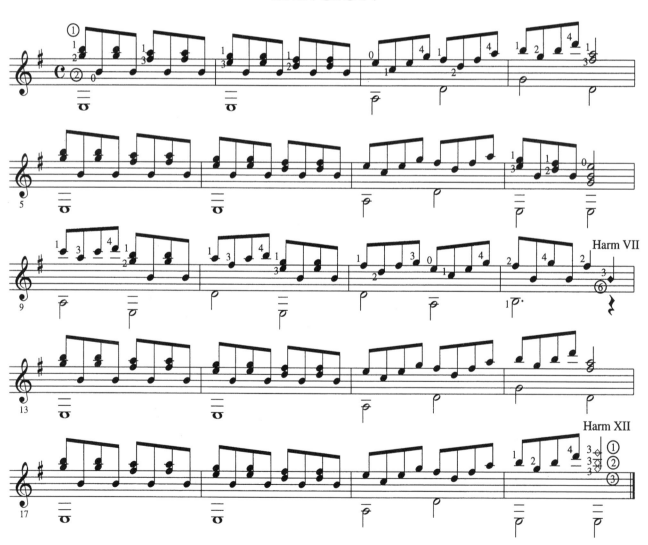

Notes on the Third String

Memorize:

G A B C D E F G

Fret: 0 2 4 5 7 9 10 12

Practice Scale #3

Exercise #14

Exercise #15 (Bach)

Exercise #16 (Hymn)

Practice Tip:

It is often helpful to rest the right-hand thumb or fingers on the strings when they are not in use. This technique is called *planting*. Aside from the dampening benefits, it provides great stability, security, and accuracy for the right hand. Planting is especially helpful in fast scale and arpeggio passages. The planted finger or thumb acts as an anchor or "handrail" for the rest of the hand. This is a variation of the planting technique described in Volume One, where you plant in preparation for an arpeggio.

Dampening

Dampening, to review, is the term that describes stopping unwanted notes from ringing—either notes previously played or ones caused by sympathetic vibrations. Sometimes these notes can be used to your advantage or make no consequence at all; but other times they cause a distracting dissonance. A general technique for dampening bass strings is to lay the right-hand thumb down so it touches the 6th, 5th, and 4th strings all at once. This will take care of most sympathetic vibrations. You will often need to stop a bass note from ringing at the exact same time you need to play another bass note. This is a somewhat difficult but often necessary technique.

In the following two examples, the first bass note needs to be stopped as you play the second. After each example you will find three alternative techniques to accomplish the dampening:

1. Use back of thumb to stop E as you play **A**.
2. Set thumb on 6th string immediately after you play **A**.
3. Use left hand.

1. Use rest stroke with thumb.
2. Set thumb on 5th string immediately after you play **E**.
3. Use left hand or a finger of the right hand.

To dampen a higher adjacent treble string, slightly flatten a left-hand finger. You may also set a right-hand finger on any treble string.

INTERLUDE

Try dampening the open bass strings by setting the thumb down on the previously played bass note (technique #2). This action will also provide security for your right hand.

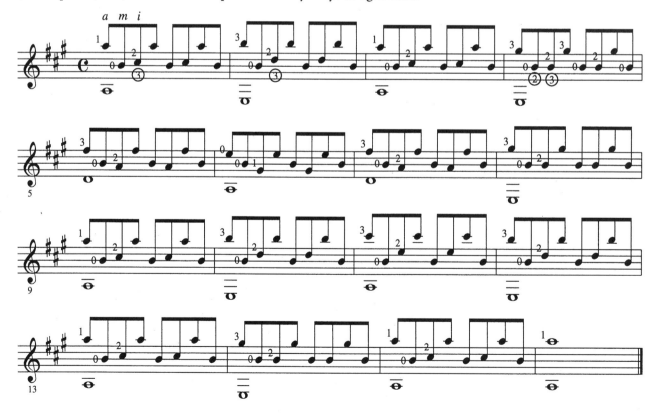

24

FRENCH LULLABY

DAVID BRANDON

Practice Tip:

Your progress on the guitar is similar to stretching a rubberband. It is easy to stretch at first, but the farther you stretch it, the harder it becomes to do so. The last refinements you add to your playing may be the most tedious. Stretching that last 5% out of your playing to make it 100% of what you want can be the most difficult.

More Work on the Treble Strings

Exercise #17 (Dvorak) This study is excellent for the practice of vibrato.

RUSSIAN FOLK SONG

TRADITIONAL

TARANTELLA

D.C. al Coda

CAROL OF THE BELLS

M. Leontovich
arr. D. Brandon

This effective little piece imitates the sound of a choir and demonstrates the wonderful *polyphonic* (two or more musical lines played simultaneously) quality of the guitar. One voice starts, then a second enters, then a third, and finally a fourth. Listen to each voice separately and make sure to let each note ring for its full value.

Notes on the Fourth String

Memorize:

D E F G A B C D

Fret: 0 2 3 5 7 9 10 12

Practice Scale #4

Exercise #18

Exercise #19 (Lehár)

Exercise #20 (Humperdinck)

Practice Tip:
Left-hand squeaks on bass strings are annoying unwanted noises. In fact, many non-guitarists judge guitar players by the number of squeaks they make! Try to avoid these by lifting your left-hand finger straight off the string when shifting and quickly setting it down again in the next position. If you must leave a finger on a string for a slide, use the side or fleshy part of the fingertip below the callus to ride the string. This will minimize the noise.

PRELUDE IN E MINOR

This prelude is based on the interval of a tenth. The second string B functions as a pedal tone. Use the repeated *i* finger on this note to produce a more consistent sound. Try to avoid excessive left-hand noise. It might be helpful to practice the tenths in this piece without the open pedal tone to concentrate on making quiet left-hand shifts.

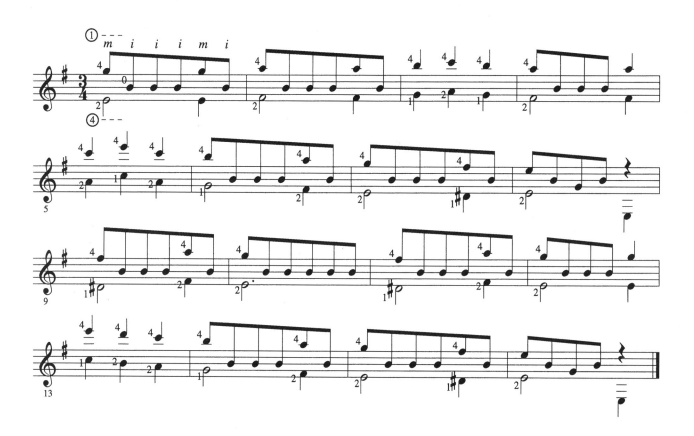

Success vs. Excellence

I suggest that you pursue a commitment to personal *excellence* rather than *success*, based on your own God-given potential. *Success* and *excellence* are often competing ideals. Being *successful* does not necessarily mean you will be *excellent*, and being *excellent* does not necessarily mean you will be *successful*. *Success* is attaining or achieving cultural goals, which elevates one's importance in the society in which he lives. *Excellence* is the pursuit of quality in one's work and effort, whether the culture recognizes it or not. I once asked Segovia how many hours a day he practiced. He responded, "Christopher, I practice 2½ hours in the morning and 2½ hours every afternoon." I thought to myself, "If Segovia needs to practice five hours every day, how much more do I need to practice?"

Success seeks status, power, prestige, wealth, and privilege. *Excellence* is internal—seeking satisfaction in having done your best. *Success* is external—how you have done in comparison to others. *Excellence* is how you have done in relation to your own potential. For me, *success* seeks to please men, but *excellence* seeks to please God.

Success grants its rewards to a few, but is the dream of the multitudes. *Excellence* is available to all, but is accepted only by a few. *Success* engenders a fantasy and a compulsive groping for the pot of gold at the end of the rainbow. *Excellence* brings us down to reality with a deep gratitude for the promise of joy when we do our best. *Excellence* cultivates principles, character, and integrity. *Success* may be cheap, and you can take shortcuts to get there. *You will pay the full price for excellence*; it is never discounted. *Excellence* will always cost you everything, but it is the most lasting and rewarding ideal. What drives you—*success* or *excellence?*

SCARBOROUGH FAIR

ENGLISH FOLK SONG
arr. D. Brandon

The ending of this piece echoes the melody in harmonics, reminiscent of the last drops of rain after an English shower.

Notes on the Fifth String

Notes on the Sixth String

Memorize:

Fret: 0   1   3   5   7   8   10   12

Practice Scale #6

Exercise #25

Exercise #26 (Grieg)

Exercise #27 (Tchaikowsky)

Exercise #28 (Saint-Saens)

At this point it would be very helpful to practice groups of the same three notes on each string. Concentrate on the names and positions of each note. Play the following exercise with every consecutive three-note combination. In other words, play the EFG sequence on each string, as the exercise shows. Notice they do not have to be in the same octave. Then play ABC on every string, etc. Also play the three notes in reverse order.

Exercise #29

More Work on the Bass Strings

Exercise #30

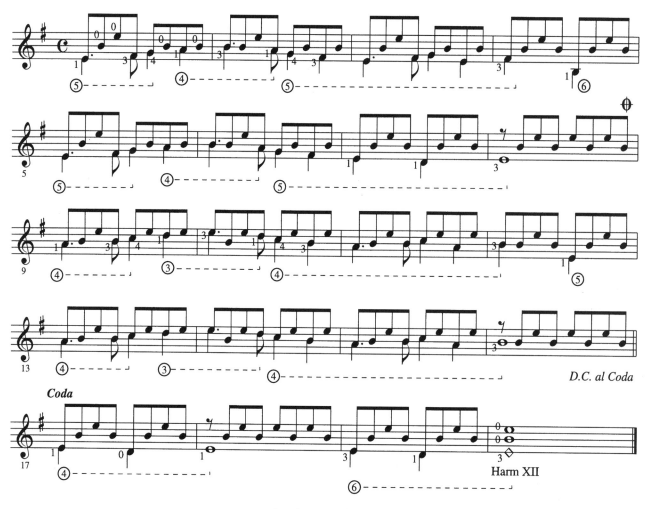

Sightreading

Sightreading is a very useful skill to develop. It makes trying and learning new pieces easier, and is essential for impromptu ensemble playing. Here are some ideas to help you improve your reading ability:

- Quantity practice is essential. Read through as much material as possible and do not try to perfect each piece. Play through them two or three times at the most. After that, you are no longer sightreading.

- Keep your eyes on the music and read at a consistent tempo, slow enough to play most of the piece right. Practice difficult rhythms separately by tapping them out or by making all notes the same pitch.

- Continually look ahead (even a full measure) and do not go back. Think about what you are going to do, instead of what you are actually doing. You will eventually recognize chords as you do words, and a musical phrase becomes equivalent to a sentence.

- Create your own sightreading exercises. Take some manuscript paper and jot down notes in random order that give you trouble. Set an even tempo and read through them. Also try the easier exercises from Volume One and play them in different positions on the neck.

- Check out guitar methods or anthologies from the library for extra practice. Clarinet or violin methods are also good because of similar range and clef, and they do not contain guitar fingerings. For extra practice in flat key signatures, read the treble clef from a book of hymns.

- Play ensemble music (duets, trios, quartets).

Mastering the Fingerboard

Here is a simple system for learning the notes on the guitar quickly and thoroughly. It is well worth the few minutes each day to become fluent on the fingerboard. These exercises can be done by yourself or with a teacher or fellow student. Follow the system step-by-step at your own pace, and proceed only when you have mastered each step.

1) String by string:

a) Learn the natural notes on each string up to the 12th fret. Starting with the 6th string, name different notes randomly as you play them. Proceed to the 5th string, etc.

b) Learn the chromatic notes on each string. Starting with the 6th string, randomly name notes sharp/flat, then flat/sharp. By naming both sharp and flat, and in reverse order, you will learn to recognize both equally.

c) Mix natural and chromatic notes. Starting with the 6th string, randomly say and play every single note. Proceed string by string.
(Note: At this point, you will have learned every

note on the guitar, open–12th fret. The next steps will reinforce what you have learned.)

2) Fret by fret: Choose a fret and randomly name and play all the notes on that fret. Cover all frets 1 thru 12.

3) Say a note and play it on every string, starting with the 6th. For example, play one F on every string.

4) Put your finger down anywhere on the neck and name the note.

5) Explore higher frets above the 12th, especially the more frequently used treble strings. Since the notes are the same, but an octave higher than the lower fingerboard, it will not take long to learn the notes beyond the 12th fret.

More Sightreading Practice

LESSON IN A MINOR

NAPOLEON COSTE

35

LESSON IN A MAJOR

NAPOLEON COSTE

MOTO PERPETUO (excerpt)

NICOLO PAGANINI

For sightreading only, this piece may be practiced in sections. Try playing in a variety of positions on the neck.

Performance Anxiety

Performance anxiety (stage fright) is a potential problem that can be disastrous to any performance. Andrés Segovia acknowledged that a guitarist could lose up to 50% of his technique due to nerves. He even remarked, "When I go to a concert I am always nervous; then when I have to begin a concert I am ready to cancel it; but when I have finished a concert, I would like to begin again." Stagefright can be overcome, though, and you can learn to use the excitement produced by the expectation of a concert to your advantage.

Everyone has a different approach to conquering performance anxiety. American film composer John Williams once related to me this story about the great cellist Gregor Piatagorsky. In a conversation about the dilemma of stagefright, a friend of Piatagorsky suggested that backstage before the concert the cellist should just tell himself "I am the great Gregor Piatagorsky" and he would not have any problem with nerves. Piatagorsky replied, "That is what I already do. The problem is…I do not believe myself!" This humorous anecdote shows to what extreme we sometimes go in dealing with this problem.

One key to overcoming stagefright is preparation. Long-term preparation would start taking place when you first schedule a performance (or even before). Short-term preparation would be effective the day of the performance. By using the following ideas, you should gain insight to help you deliver your best performance that is not hampered by nerves, but rather charged by enthusiasm.

Long-Term Preparation

- Practice effectively. This means working out the details of the music and your performance in advance. There is no substitute for being adequately prepared.

- Choose a program within your capability. Start with a secure piece that will allow you to feel comfortable on stage. Plan stage entrances, bows, and announcements as much as possible prior to the performance.

- Simulate performance conditions. If possible, do a practice concert. Take advantage of every performance opportunity to refine your performing skills. Learn to play cold without warming up. You might also try tape recording yourself.

- Note several sections of each piece of music that you could start from should a memory lapse occur in concert. If one does occur, jump to one of these sections and keep going. Do not dwell on the memory lapse, but think about expressing the music.

Short-Term Preparation

- Arrive at the performance venue early to get comfortable with the stage, lighting, chair, and sound of the hall.

- Warm up, but do not overdo. In general, play a little slower with perhaps less volume, saving energy for the concert. Do not give your best performance in the dressing room.

- Do not be analytical about the music backstage. At this point you should think in more general terms.

> **Practice Tip:**
> It is important to play pieces of music as a whole, then later go back and correct mistakes. Do not stop every time you make a mistake, as this habit could cause you to do the same in concert.

Performance Anxiety (cont.)

During Performance

- Consciously relax as practiced and concentrate on playing the music beautifully.

- If you make a mistake, keep going and continue to try your best. Do not let your feelings dictate your attitude, but focus on the music.

> **Practice Tip:**
> If you cannot warm up before a performance, massaging or exercising your hands together keeps them warm and ready to play. If you are able to hold the guitar but must remain quiet, such as in a television appearance, I find it helpful to exercise the left hand by pressing the strings down with firmness in various patterns on the fingerboard.

- Sometimes you must take musical and technical chances in performance to play something extraordinarily beautiful or exciting. I have seen Segovia "play on the edge"—taking the chance of sacrificing slight technical accuracies for the most exhilarating performance. As wonderful as flawless technique may be, it is genuine musicality that will truly move an audience.

For my personal note on this subject, see p. 135.

Christopher Parkening and co-author David Brandon in concert.

Left-Hand Fingering Principles

In his method for guitar, Fernando Sor said to consider fingering an art. As you may have observed in some of the previous exercises, it is possible to play a passage in more than one spot on the neck for tonal variety. It is not uncommon to spend a lot of time experimenting with different fingerings for a passage to decide which one is best musically and technically. As a general rule, use the most natural fingering unless a more difficult one gives a better musical interpretation, i.e., tonal variety, more beautiful phrasing, etc.

Below you will find a melody from Volume One with a variety of different fingerings. An evaluation of the fingering accompanies every passage. Play each example to analyze its strengths and weaknesses.

1) All notes on same string—consistent in sound and good for right hand; brightest tone.

2) All notes on same string; medium tone—best overall. Vibrato can be used on all three notes.

3) All notes on same string; thickest tone—can be somewhat muddy. Vibrato can be used on all three notes.

4) Contains string crossings—not consistent in sound but good for some situations. Also harder for the right hand.

5) Contains string crossings (see #4).

6) Contains string crossings; awkward reach.

7) Contains string crossings; somewhat awkward for the left hand.

8) Cross-string fingering allows strings to ring, achieving a harp-like effect.

In fingering music you have to consider context, other voices, tempo, musical style, and whether to add slurs. Ultimately you will find a balance between technical and musical elements. It is important to be able to play a fingering up to tempo and in context before you judge its merit. Also, do not be afraid to change a fingering as your musical tastes and technical abilities change. You will constantly want to re-evaluate your fingering of music. Bad fingering will tend to wear on you. Through many years of playing and teaching the same piece, Segovia often improved a piece by changing the fingering. I consider Segovia's fingerings a musical art form and a great study in themselves. Aside from that, use editor's suggestions as a guide, but allow yourself to personalize a piece with your own fingerings.

Accuracy and Control

Proper placement and control of finger movement is essential for accurate playing with minimal mistakes. It is necessary to obtain a balanced left-hand position (fig. 5), playing directly on the fingertips. (fig. 6) Try to economize the movement of the fingers by keeping them close to the strings when not in use. The following two exercises will help you develop control and economy of motion. The first is monophonic (only one voice) and should be played on all strings in a variety of positions. I suggest setting all the fingers down on the string in proper playing position (fig. 6)

before you begin the exercise. Lift the 2nd, 3rd, and 4th fingers slightly, and you will be ready to play. Use as little movement as possible, keeping the 1st finger down all the time. Leave the 2nd and 3rd fingers down after they have been played whenever possible.

Exercise #18 is polyphonic. You must allow one note to ring while playing the other three. Again, practice this in a variety of positions, and even try increasing the string spread. (For example, play on strings one and three.) Play both exercises slowly so as to fully concentrate on control and accuracy.

Fig. 5 Proper left-hand position.

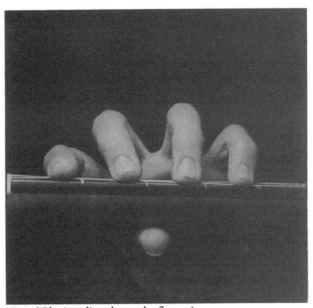

Fig. 6 Playing directly on the fingertips.

Exercise #31

Exercise #32

Practice Tip:

Making progress on the guitar is like hiking up a mountain. You hike up as far as you can on one trail and then when it ends, you must backtrack down to find another trail that leads even higher. In other words, when working on a technical problem, you may have to take one step backward in order to take two steps forward.

Unrealistic Progress: Actual Progress:

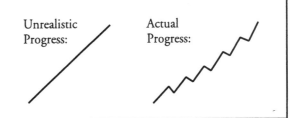

Moveable Scales

Practicing scales is a fundamental aspect in the development of technique for every musician. Scales are the building blocks of music, and practicing them will help cultivate tone, control, dexterity, speed, and stamina. In fact, Segovia stated, "The practice of scales enables one to solve a greater number of technical problems in a shorter period of time than the study of any other exercise." Below are four moveable scale patterns—two major and two minor. Because they contain no open stings, these scales can be played in any key by starting on the appropriate root note. For instance, the first pattern in C major on the third fret can be changed to D major by starting on the fifth fret. For technical practice, I suggest playing each scale ascending and descending starting on frets 3,4,5,6,7 and then back 6,5,4,3. Start slowly, play evenly, and increase speed gradually for each new key.

More practice advice for scales:

- Decide on a specific goal to accomplish while practicing a scale. Ten minutes of concentrated practice covering a certain aspect can be more beneficial than an hour of mindlessly running scales.

C Major

- Try different right-hand fingering combinations: *im, mi, ia, ai, ma, am, pi,* etc. Some patterns, such as *ma,* are not feasible for most players in a high-speed concert run; however, they do help gain independence for some situations.

G Major

- Play rest stroke and free stroke. Also try a light rest stroke. This is a hybrid stroke—a rest stroke with a free stroke feel and speed.

C Minor

- Experiment with different angles of the right hand and fingers. Also be sure your nails are filed properly.

- Many players find it beneficial to rest the thumb on the 6th string as an anchor. Others change the anchor string as they ascend the scale. This is also helpful for dampening unwanted ringing strings.

G Minor

- Practice preparing each stroke. Start out by thinking of each scale note as an eighth note with an eighth rest in between. On the rest, prepare the next right-hand finger by planting it on the string in preparation to play the next note. Proceed to lengthen the played note and shorten the rest/preparation time.

- After good preparation is achieved, practice synchronization of right and left hands. Ideally, fingers of both hands should move at exactly the same moment. This will achieve a perfectly legato sound with no perceptible break between notes.

- Extract scale passages from actual pieces and use them as exercises. For example, I often use the scales from Rodrigo's *Concierto de Aranjuez* for scale practice. In this way, I polish part of a concert piece while refining technique. For more work on scales, I recommend Segovia's *Diatonic Major and Minor Scales* (Columbia Music).

Scale Variations

Try applying the following variations to the prededing scales for extra practice and increased endurance.

Repeated Notes:

Sequences:

Dotted Rhythms:

Speed Techniques

The following exercise will help demonstrate practice techniques used to gain speed. First learn and memorize the passage by playing it slowly and accurately. Gradually increase the speed as you gain confidence with it. Next, apply the following ideas to help maximize your own speed potential.

To achieve speed, practice the scale in short segments. Just as a runner who can run a short sprint trains for a longer race, you can practice small bursts of speed while gradually increasing the distance. Isolate the first pattern of four eighth notes to practice. Add one extra note also, giving you a downbeat—a place to land. This is similar to the runner who runs *through* the finish line instead of stopping at it. He maintains his momentum until the end. Practice this pattern of five notes as fast as possible, only *accurately*. Repeat this over and over, increasing the speed until you have gone as fast as you can play without mistakes. Then start a little slower and try the next pattern, gradually increasing the speed to as fast as you can play with accuracy. Finally, add both patterns together to make a complete measure plus the downbeat of the next measure. Continue this process over the entire passage.

A metronome is of great value when striving for speed. It is equivalent to a stop-watch used by a runner in training. It will help you stay in tempo and also monitor your progress. Concert guitarists, depending on the difficulty of the scale, reach speeds between 138–172 (four notes per click).

For left-hand accuracy, be sure to play directly on the fingertips, keep the fingers close to the strings without excessive motion, and maintain a balanced hand position. You must also have the right hand in the correct position *with the nails filed properly* to achieve maximum speed.

You may wish to practice the right hand alone. Practice the first short segment in Ex. #33 staying on the same note, that is, four plus one A's. Then practice eight plus one A's, etc. When you have achieved a certain degree of speed, add the left-hand changes to obtain synchronization between both hands.

You might also find it helpful to start at the end of the exercise and work backward. Play the last five notes (ending on the downbeat), then the last nine, etc. This is similar to a runner backing up from the finish line.

Practice Tip:
Speed can be measured, just like a 100-meter dash. However, there is a more desirable musical goal that we should strive for—one that cannot be measured. It is the musicality and feeling of the music we play. Use speed to attain that goal, but never let it take the place of beautiful playing.

Exercise #33

Special Effects

There are numerous interesting techniques on the guitar used to create special *timbres* (tone colors) or sound effects. Natural harmonics were covered earlier and artificial harmonics will follow this section. Here are many of the others:

Pizzicato (*pizz.*)—This technique involves muffling the strings (usually bass) with the side of the right hand near the bridge as you play the notes with the side of the thumb (all flesh). (fig. 7) Set your hand on the bridge somewhat parallel to it as if you were to give it a "karate chop." Bring it over on the strings to muffle them slightly when plucked. (fig.8) The closer the hand is moved toward the soundhole, the more muffled the sound. Conversely, the more of your hand you rest on the bridge, the less muffled the sound. The right amount of pressure takes practice and you may have to alter your position depending on which string you desire to mute. Pizzicato notes can be plucked with the fingers as well. Segovia also created a pizzicato-like sound by using the back portion of his thumb (see picture) for instant dampening of the bass strings, as in his recording of *Tonadilla* (*La Maya de Goya*) by Granados. (fig. 9)

Fig. 7 Pizzicato shown from the front.

Fig. 8 Pizzicato shown from neck view.

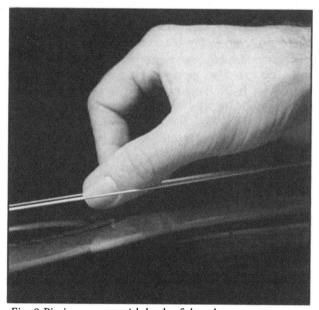

Fig. 9 Pizzicato mute with back of thumb.

Glissando (Slide)—In addition to the slur, another way of sounding a second note without plucking it is to *slide*. To do this, move your finger between two notes while firmly pressing the string. It is sometimes desirable to use a slight glissando (also called *portamento*) between two notes and to actually play the second note. This is notated with an added grace note but is often left to the discretion of the performer.

Ponticello (*pont.*)—This term describes the brittle, metallic sound achieved by plucking the strings near the bridge, usually with the center of the nail. (fig. 10) This quality was used extensively in my recording of the *Allemande* by Dowland (transcription on p. 76).

Dolce (also marked *sul tasto*)—the sweet warm tone achieved by playing over the sound hole, usually with the side of the nail. (fig. 11) The term *naturale* indicates the return to a more normal sound. For a more in depth discussion of tone color, refer to Appendix A.

Fig. 10 Ponticello position.

Fig. 11 Dolce position.

Tambora—This drum-like effect involves bouncing the right-hand thumb (sometimes the fingers) on the strings near the bridge. (figs. 12 and 13) By bouncing quickly, but firmly, the strings will sound.

An example of the tambora technique may be found in my recording of *Simple Gifts*.

Fig. 12 Tambora with the thumb.

Fig. 13 Tambora with the fingers.

Rasgueado—This is the Spanish term for strumming the guitar and is used extensively in flamenco guitar music. Though not used as often in classical guitar music, it is nevertheless a necessary technique to master. Examples of rasgueados in the classical guitar repertoire include the opening of Rodrigo's famous *Concierto de Aranjuez*, Turina's *Seviallanas*, and Falla's *The Miller's Dance*. There are many patterns, but a basic rasgueado is a brush across the strings starting with the little finger (notated *c*, *e*, or *L*) and ending with *i*—as in *cami*. For added clarity and strength, the principle of resistance is applied (similar to snapping your finger). You create tension by locking each finger (*cami*) behind the other and then releasing them in succession. (fig. 14) Occasionally the thumb is involved (either up or down) with repeated rasgueados. The index finger is often used alone in single strokes back and forth while the thumb rests on the sixth string. The first joint should remain relaxed on the upstroke. Rasgueados are usually notated by arrows which reflect the direction of the stroke. An arrow drawn from the 6th string to the 1st would indicated a strum in that same direction.

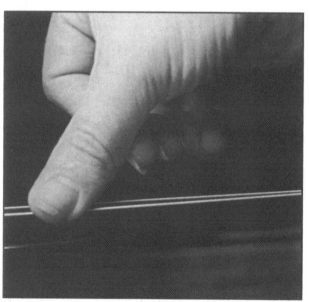

Fig. 14 Preparation of the rasgueado.

Golpe—This is a knock or tap anywhere on the guitar—often near or on the bridge or on the face of the guitar. Different fingers and positions produce a variety of percussive effects. Examples of this technique may be found in Granados' *Intermezzo* and the Renaissance dance, *Watkin's Ale* (*Virtuoso Duets*).

Tremolo—One of the most intriguing effects, this technique especially captivates audiences. It literally means a rapid repetition of the same note, the way a mandolin or a balalaika is commonly played. But in classical guitar, it generally refers to a repeated melody note *with* an added bass line, giving the illusion of two instruments playing together. It is usually played *pami* (as in the famous *Recuerdos de la Alhambra* by Tárrega), although *pmi* and *piami* are also common variations. Here are some tips to help master this difficult technique:

- The tremolo should be very even with the melody notes coming out in volume over the bass line. It should be fast enough to create the illusion of a sustained note.

- Start by practicing with the thumb on a bass string and the fingers on the first string. Play slowly at first. Try planting the *a* finger on the next melody note as you play the bass note with the thumb. In other words, set the *a* finger on the first string in position at the same moment the thumb strikes the bass string.

- Nails should be evenly filed so as to cross the strings with the same amount of resistance. This will create evenness in both rhythm and sound.

- Be sure that the right-hand knuckles are kept parallel to the string and tilt the hand slightly to the right to favor the *a* finger.

- To avoid a "gallop" or unevenness, start slowly with a metronome and work to increase speed.

- Once comfortable with the tremolo technique, practice one pattern plus the next bass note as fast and evenly as possible. Gradually add more patterns to increase endurance.

- Use different accents or reverse the pattern (for practice only) to correct unevenness.

- To help hear the rhythmic definition, try putting a cloth under the strings next to the bridge to dampen the sound slightly.

Other composers who have used the tremolo technique effectively include Ponce, Tansman, Barrios, and Castelnuovo-Tedesco.

Notation of Special Effects

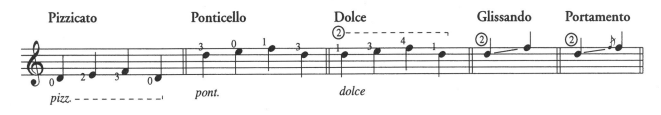

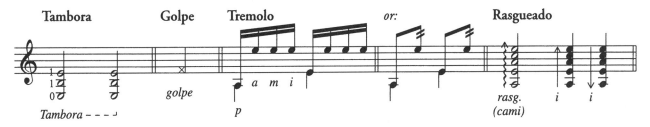

SAKURA

JAPANESE FOLK SONG

The many special effects used in this piece help capture the essence of oriental music and its exotic instruments.

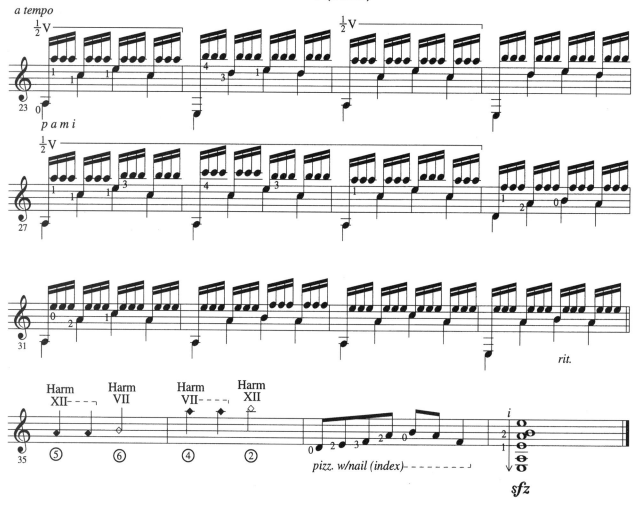

Artificial Harmonics

Harmonics (see page 21) can also be produced by the right hand alone by lightly touching a string 12 frets higher than a fretted note with the index finger and plucking it with either the thumb (fig. 15), ring finger (fig. 16), or the little finger. It is helpful to spread out the plucking finger and the node (touching) finger to achieve a clear, bell-like sound. The harmonic will sound an octave higher than the fretted note. This allows you to make any note a harmonic. Like natural harmonics, artificial ones can be produced at distances other than 12 frets, such as 7 or 19. Many unique effects can be created with harmonics, and it is enjoyable to experiment with this technique.

In the following piece, the entire melody is played with artificial harmonics. I suggest first learning the piece in natural notes and then adding harmonics when you are comfortable with the left-hand fingerings. When first learning the piece without harmonics, pluck the melody notes with only the *a* finger and the bass notes with the thumb, just as you would with artificial harmonics.

An advanced arrangement of this piece, entitled *La Filla del Marxant*, appears on my EMI recording, *A Tribute to Segovia*.

> **Practice Tip:**
> Your music will generally go through four stages as you take it from sightreading to performance:
>
> **Repeat**–Play through the piece over and over to learn it, working through the technical difficulties.
>
> **Remember**–Memorize the music and fingerings.
>
> **Refine**–Smooth out technical problems and polish interpretation.
>
> **Review**–Once mastered, review the piece frequently to maintain it as part of your repertoire.

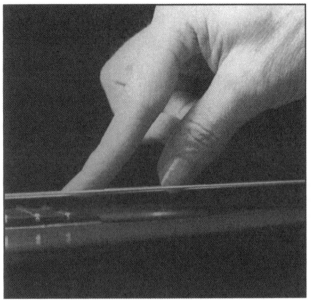

Fig. 15 Artificial harmonic plucked with the thumb.

Fig. 16 Artificial harmonic plucked by the ring finger.

CATALONIAN FOLK SONG

Melody in Artificial Harmonics...

Tuning Tips

Tuning the instrument can be one of the most frustrating aspects of playing the guitar. This is due in part to the fact that even under the best conditions, it is physically impossible to perfectly tune the instrument. The very nature of our *well-tempered* or *equal-tempered* tuning system means that we will be equally out of tune in each key. To compensate for this on the guitar you should tune to the key of the piece you are playing (called *temper-tuning*). This involves checking the prominent chords in the piece and reaching a balance or compromise between them. Here are some suggestions for refining your tuning:

- A good chord to check tuning is the open E major chord and the full bar version of that chord (making it A major on the 5th fret, B major on the 7th, etc.). The outer strings contain the root of the chord, the next to outer strings have the fifth, and on the innermost strings you find another root and the third of the chord (on the third string). The roots and fifth are very stable intervals, but the third presents a special problem since the fretted note always sounds higher than the natural harmonic overtone occurring on that note. Do not tune the 3rd string too flat, or it will be out of tune in other chords.

- It is wise to check different voicings of chords in the key of the piece you will play. Check a first position chord as well as voicings or inversions in the middle and upper parts of the neck.

- Tuning by octaves can also be beneficial. Start with the open E's and the 4th string E. Then tune the open A with the 3rd string, 2nd fret and the 1st string, 5th fret. Lastly, check other octaves such as D, B, G, etc. Depending on how trained your ear is, you could even check the interval of a fifth between the 1st and 5th strings open.

- A string has less chance of slipping flat if you tune up to pitch from below rather than down from above.

- The string may sometimes stick in the nut of the guitar when tuning up or down from another tuning. To cause the string to go a bit lower, stretch the string slightly by pulling it with the right hand towards the bridge. (Do not pull out away from the guitar because this might cause too much tension on the bridge.) Then re-adjust the tuning. To slightly raise a string's pitch, press on the string above the nut. These adjustments may also be needed when using a capo or when making very fine corrections that are too sensitive for the tuning pegs.

- Tune quietly and quickly on stage in order not to disrupt the performance. Be sure to check some of the chords in the piece.

- Be prepared to adjust tuning within a piece while you are performing. Often there are short breaks that are long enough to reach up and make a minor alteration. Practice this first, and plan possible places in your pieces for tuning adjustments. This is especially important when playing in altered tunings (see following section), where the newly tuned string will have a tendency to change pitch. An excellent time to practice this is when you first change your strings. As you play your music, reach up and tune the strings while you are playing without actually stopping. Learn to make the adjustments as quickly and discreetly as possible.

Tuning Tips (cont.)

- When tuning down to an altered tuning, bring the string down further than it needs to go and let it set there while you check the other strings. Then bring it up to pitch. This will help prevent slippage during the next piece.

- You also can push a note flat or pull a note sharp by pushing or pulling parallel to the string with the fretting finger. This works especially well in higher positions, where intonation is more likely to be a problem. Vibrato can also help establish a pitch.

- Some guitarists accidently bend strings with their left hand, causing them to play out of tune. Be sure to press the string straight down with the left-hand finger so as to not alter the pitch.

- Tuning by harmonics is a common tuning practice, and while not totally reliable, it is helpful for matching just one string against another (see diagram). It is also the easiest way to tune the guitar to the tuning fork (A 440). Match the 5th string, 5th fret or 4th string, 7th fret to the fork. The tone of a harmonic is closer to the fork than that of a fretted note.

A440	=	5th string, 5th fret
5th string, 7th fret	=	6th string, 5th fret
5th string, 5th fret	=	4th string, 7th fret
4th string, 5th fret	=	3rd string, 7th fret
5th string, 7th fret	=	1st string open
6th string, 7th fret	=	2nd string open

- Battery operated tuners are all right for general tuning, but they will not temper tune the guitar for the key of your piece. They are fine, however, for people developing their ear while learning to play guitar. A good ear and sense of pitch may take some time to develop.

- Bad strings will often impair intonation. Check your string by comparing the 12th fret harmonic to the same note fretted. These should be the same. If there is a discrepancy, consider replacing the string. You may have to settle for one that is slightly out of tune at the 12th fret, but you will get to know your instrument and choice of strings and will be able to reach a compromise. Other problems that can hinder tuning are a warped neck, worn frets, and misaligned frets (rare).

Practice Tip:
It is important to be able to play a piece at a variety of tempos. When you are cold on stage or have not been able to warm-up prior to the performance, you may wish to take a little slower tempo. You should also be able to play a piece a somewhat faster than needed, giving you a bit of reserve. This is especially important when playing ensemble music or concertos with orchestras. The conductor may choose a different tempo than where you have normally practiced the piece.

Low D Tuning

The next piece requires that the 6th string be tuned a whole step lower to D. This pitch will be an octave lower than the 4th string open, so it is best to match it to that string. For an easy check, the 12th fret harmonic on the 6th string should be in unison with the 4th string open. Also, the 6th string, 7th fret will now match the 5th string open (both natural notes). With this tuning change, play the 6th string notes two frets higher than they would normally be played. (You can think of them in relation to the 4th string, only one octave lower.) There are many alternate tunings on the guitar, but this is by far the most common.

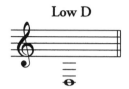

PRELUDIO

ANONYMOUS

Practice Tip:
My father used to have me play a passage seven times in a row perfectly at tempo before he considered it mastered. If I made a mistake anywhere, even on the last time through, I would have to start over again until I could do seven consecutive times without mistakes. Apply this type of discipline to your practicing for maximum technical accuracy.

Paganini's *Theme and Variation* from *Caprice #24* provides some advanced work with slurs. The theme focuses on hammer-ons and the variation utilizes pull-offs. It is an excellent workout for the left hand.

THEME AND VARIATION
(from Caprice #24)

Niccolo Paganini

Ornamentation

Early music before 1750 (Renaissance and Baroque) was often decorated with embellishments called ornaments. Many of these were not even notated in the score, and much has been written regarding style and practice. Here is a very general and simplified guide to ornamentation. Although style and tradition are important considerations, I feel that the performer should ultimately do what sounds best on his individual instrument.

In Baroque music, trills generally start on the upper note. The trilled note should come from the scale and the key of the piece, unless an accidental is added. The duration of a trill is subject to the tempo and performer's interpretation. In all examples, the bass notes are played with the ornament.

Each period of music had its own conventions, so it is impossible to be dogmatic on the execution of these ornaments. It is often helpful to study theory, musicianship, and interpretation with other instrumentalists (non-guitarists) or with early music specialists. Segovia often encouraged students in the study of music in general, saying, "You must love the music more than you love the guitar."

Technical Note: Some ornaments (such as trills and mordents) are sometimes played cross-string rather than slurred. To execute this, rapidly alternate the trilled notes fingered on two consecutive strings.

Advanced Bar Techniques

The next piece uses the technique of a *hinge bar.* (fig. 17) The example in the photo, on the first fret, is notated Ih. The first string is fretted by the first finger as if it were a full-length bar, but the finger is angled away from the bass strings to allow the open D to ring. This facilitates movement to the next chord, where the first finger lays down on all the strings to form a full bar.

Other special bar techniques also exist. Occasionally you will need to use a *partial bar* on inside strings and leave open strings above and below it. This is done by flattening the index finger and bending *backwards* at the first joint. This bar is often notated with a bracket next to the barred notes. Bars using fingers other than the index are also usually notated in this manner. (fig. 18)

Another unusual bar technique is the *cross fret bar,* whereby the index finger bars across two frets simultaneously. (fig. 19) An example

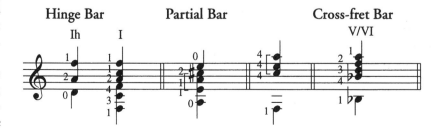

of this technique may be found in Rick Foster's transcription of *Sheep May Safely Graze* (*Parkening Plays Bach*). Here the index finger slants such that the bottom half depresses the treble strings and the top half of the finger depresses the bass strings a fret higher. This is notated by two Roman numerals with a slash between them.

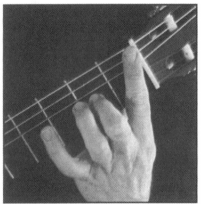

Fig. 17 Hinge Bar.

Fig. 18 Partial Bar with 4th finger.

Fig. 19 Cross-fret Bar.

BIANCO FIORE

ANONYMOUS

Because of the Allegro tempo, the trills in this piece are generally performed starting on the lower note. This transcription appears on *The Artistry of Christopher Parkening*.

Interval Studies

Here are three excellent studies to help in the mastery of playing polyphonic music. They contain three of the most frequently used intervals in classical music. After learning the 3rds and 6ths as they are written in the key of C, try adding one sharp (on F) to play them in the key of G. Do this for all key signatures. Also try playing tenths (a third plus an octave) and thirteenths (a sixth plus an octave). Practice the exercises ascending and descending. Be sure to play directly on the fingertips, keep the fingers close to the strings without excessive motion, and maintain a balanced left-hand position. For more work on 3rds and 6ths, practice *Study #12* (Op. 6, no. 6 and *Study #13* (Op. 6, no. 9) by Sor (ed. Segovia).

Left-Hand Shifts

There are two main types of left-hand shifts on the neck: those that can use guide fingers (keeping a finger on the string during the shift) and those that can not. Regardless of the type of shift, try to keep your hand in a balanced position. This involves moving from the arm and keeping the fingers close to the strings. If you have a difficult shift along the neck, you may find it helpful to isolate the passage and create an exercise out of it. The following example contains a difficult chord shift from the 2nd to the 7th position. (Ex. A) Although you have the advanatge of a guide finger, the fingering is somewhat awkward. To break the problem down into smaller pieces, first practice the change of fingering *in the same position.* (Ex. B) Here the guide finger functions simply as a pivot finger. Next, practice shifting just one fret or two. Finally, resume practice of the full shift to the 7th position.

For shifts without a guide finger, I suggest momentarily riding along the inside area of the index finger opposite the first knuckle. That is, the inside of the finger remains in contact with the bottom of the neck as you shift. Keep the fingers close to the strings and in position as much as possible. Try this with Example C.

For shifts to the uppermost frets, you will need to alter your left-hand postiion somewhat. (fig. 20)

Exercise #34

Fig. 20 Left hand in extreme upper position.

Rules To Be Broken

There are a few "textbook" rules that you may come across in your study of guitar. While these principles are excellent guidelines, not all can be applied to every situation. Below you will find a few of these concepts with some suggestions of when to use them and when to ignore them.

1) *Alternate right-hand fingers on single note passages.* While this is beneficial on faster runs, sometimes using the same finger repeatedly is excellent for keeping a consistent sound.

2) *Use rest stroke on single note passages.* Rest stroke is good for many scale passages, accenting certain notes, and bringing out the melody line above an arpeggio. For most other passages, free stroke will be more legato and give more flexibility in terms of tone color. I personally use free stroke approximately 80% of the time.

3) *Keep the right hand still and move only finger joints.* This may be true for most faster passages; however, in beautiful melodic lines or for powerful chords, stiffening a finger or locking two or three together and then playing from the wrist/forearm will give the best sound. Using the full weight of the hand and forearm achieves the most power. Varying the angle of the nail gives fullness or thickness to the sound.

4) *Use the textbook sitting position.* There are so many physical variables (height of chair, footstool, size of person) that the sitting position will vary for each individual. Keep in mind the general principles and strive to balance security, relaxation, and technical accuracy with a beautiful sound.

5) *Play off the left side of the nail.* This is the standard for most natural and dolce sounds. However, the center and right side of the nail certainly produce unique effects and should be used and experimented with.

6) *Relax.* Although it is certainly desirable to be as relaxed as possible, there must be a certain amount of focused tension. Whether it is in the right-hand fingers or wrist for extra power and intensity, or in the left hand for difficult bars or slurs, there will always be a certain amount of tension that may even require building strength and endurance. Try to confine the tension to only the areas needed to produce the results.

7) *Play the music as written.* Guitar music is not always written the way it is played. Often notes are written to ring where they cannot or notated short where they should ring (as in an arpeggio). Sometimes you will find mistakes or poor editions. Base what you play on common musical sense and what sounds beautiful on guitar. For example, I have studied the compositions of composers such as Rodrigo, Castelnuovo-Tedesco, Mompou, and Torroba, and they all have personally accommodated my small changes in their music to facilitate the best expression on guitar. This also applies to transcriptions. Bach regularly transcribed and adapted works for different instruments or settings.

Practice Tip:
In general, the more stable the instrument, the more accurately you will play. For added stability, try resting the lower main bout of the guitar on the chair (padded) between your legs. This will provide five points of security: 1) on the left leg, 2) against the inside of the right leg, 3) against your chest, 4) under your right forearm, and 5) on the chair.

Twenty-Minute Workout

If you desire a quick warm-up or technical workout, try five minutes of concentrated practice in each of these four vital areas: 1) Scales 2) Arpeggios 3) Slurs 4) Stretches. Below you will find one possible example of each exercise. Customize this technical regimen to fit your own particular needs.

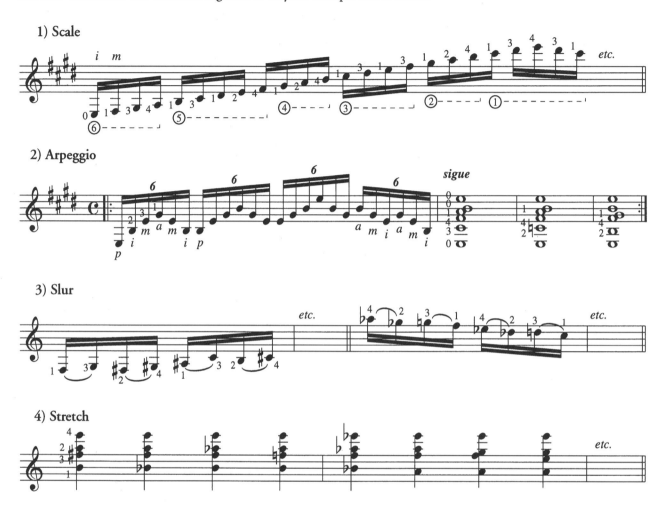

The musician's art is to send light into the depths of men's hearts.

—Robert Schumann

Interpretation of Music

I have often been asked what made Andrés Segovia a great guitarist. I believe there are four factors: 1) his great technique, 2) his uniquely beautiful sound and variety of tone colors, 3) his charisma with the audience, and 4) his musicianship (the ability to interpret the music). In fact, all of the technique learned and practiced thus far leads toward that single goal: the interpretation of music. Technique is the means, and interpretation is the end. It is breathing life into a composition, making your own personal artistic statement in a piece of music. One can look to the great recordings of Segovia to hear the beautiful nuances of color, texture, and style. He left a legacy of artistic expression which serves as model for all those who study the guitar and its infinite possibilities of interpretation. This chapter will explore many exciting aspects of this subject and give insight to the development of your own unique style.

Every musical note has four distinct qualities or characteristics: 1) *Pitch* 2) *Duration* 3) *Volume* and 4) *Tone*. Simply stated, the interpretation of music depends on how you handle each of these qualities. In other words, *emotional expression is conveyed by the amount of variation used in pitch, duration, volume, and tone*. As guitarists we are fortunate to have control over each of these qualities. Not all musicians are so blessed. Pianists, for example, have control over the duration and volume of a note, but only limited control of tone, and none over pitch. And yet look at the magnificent interpretations of the great masters such as Horowitz, Rubenstein, or Padrewsky. Just imagine how much more is possible with the versatility of the guitar. In fact, Segovia once wrote, "The beauty of the guitar resides in its soft and persuasive voice, and its poetry cannot be equaled by any other instrument." Let us now look in depth at ways to achieve variation in each of the four qualities of music. Following this discussion is a summary of these artistic devices in outline form.

1) **Pitch**—The primary means of achieving variation in the pitch is with *vibrato*. There are two variables involved here: speed and width. Generally, a slow, wide vibrato is more lyrical and a fast, short vibrato, more intense. Most often you will want to match the pulse of the vibrato to the feel of the music. This gives a consonant, harmonic effect. The use of vibrato is of great help when "singing" a phrase, and it will also increase the sustain of a note, help establish intonation, and always add expression to a passage. It would not be desirable, however, in certain bright, dance-like passages or extremely quick runs. Sometimes it is necessary to apply vibrato to an entire chord. Other times, only one note in the chord needs vibrato (usually the melody with a vertical motion).

A glissando also deviates from the pitch by subtly adding pitches between two notes. Ornaments found in early music that are left to the discretion of the performer also create new pitches, adding variation to the existing ones.

2) **Duration**—Dealing with rhythm and timing, the duration category is largely responsible for the overall feel of a piece. Even the basic decision of the proper tempo (from *Andante* to *Allegro*, etc.) deals with the duration of each note. In addition, the notes may be played *staccato* (short, detached) or *legato* (long, connected). You can speed up (*accelerando*) or slow down (*ritard* or *rallentando*). You might hold certain notes longer than others (*fermata* or *tenuto*), or even play deliberately out of time by giving extra duration to some notes and less to others (*rubato*). Cellist Pablo Casals called this "freedom with order."

Arpeggiating (rolling) a chord displaces the duration of notes and is usually done so that the melody falls directly on the beat with the other notes in the chord rapidly preceding it low to high. It is also effective to vary the speed of a rolled chord. Sometimes a faster arpeggio is desirable and other times you will want to broaden the chord. Even occasionally breaking a single bass and melody note may add beauty to a phrase.

In Baroque music you might even encounter the technique of *inegale* or *double-dotting*.

3) **Volume**—There are two main types of dynamic contrast in music: *contour* and *terrace*. Contour dynamics is *gradually* going from soft (*piano*) to loud (*forte*), or from loud to soft. It is often common to gradually get louder (*crescendo*) on a phrase that ascends in pitch and get softer

(*decrescendo* or *diminuendo*) on a descending passage. Of course, surprise is a very effective tool, so doing just the opposite of what is expected (in moderation) can sometimes create an interesting interpretation. Terrace dynamics is *abruptly* going from soft to loud or vice-versa. This got its name from the harpsichord where there are two terraces of keyboards, one louder and one softer. It is great for an echo effect in parallel passages and is often used in combination with a tone color change as well.

Volume contrast is also viewed vertically rather than horizontally. You can adjust the *balance* of a chord or passage by bringing out the melody, bass, or inner voices. This dynamic relationship between voices is crucial and can be difficult to achieve. Generally, the melody should be the loudest voice unless you want to draw attention to an interesting movement in the bass or inner voices. Occasionally the melody is in the bass line and you have to adjust your technique accordingly. Rest stroke is often used to bring out certain notes and is certainly helpful for strong accents (*sforzando*).

4) **Tone**—One of the most exciting facets of playing the guitar is the rich variety of tone colors (*timbres*) available. Virtually unparalleled in this aspect, our instrument displays a vast array of tonal textures. In fact, Ludwig van Beethoven called the guitar "a miniature orchestra in itself." The guitar even frequently imitates orchestral instruments—from the bright, piercing sounds of a trumpet to the sweet, lush sound of a string section. Although somewhat limited in its dynamic range, the guitar more than compensates for this by its generous palette of tonal colors.

There are three methods used to vary the tone color with the right hand. The most common involves the place from which the string is plucked. Near the bridge, it will produce a bright, ponticello sound. Over the soundhole, it will produce a dolce, sweet tone. Secondly, the angle of the nail on the string also has a great effect on the tone. A stroke from the center of the nail will produce a thinner bright sound; the side of the nail (or using more flesh) will create beautiful warm sounds. Last of all, and least well known, is the direction of the stroke. Plucking out away from the guitar will cause a thinner sound, and slicing the string at an angle toward the performer's left shoulder will produce a fuller sound by activating the string parallel to the face of the instrument. This not only creates the warmest tone but also produces the most power.

The left hand also plays a role in the variation of tonal contrast. Notes played in the lower positions tend to sound brighter and thinner. Notes played in the upper positions tend to be full and rich. Other left hand techniques such as slurs and slides also vary the tone slightly.

Finally, all of the special effects including harmonics, pizzicato, tambora, and rasgueado, have a dramatic effect on the variety of tone colors available on the guitar.

You will generally use a mixture of variation in all four qualities to achieve your desired interpretation. Observe the composer's markings of expression to help understand the overall concept of the piece. Then rely on your own natural musical instincts to develop your interpretation. As cellist Gregor Piatagorsky once told me, "You can learn technique, but artistic instinct is natural-born." There is only so much this book or any teacher can give to you on this subject. In fact Segovia said, "All great artists are ultimately self-taught."

Regarding the interpretation of music, Vladimir Horowitz wrote, "All music is the expression of feelings, and feelings do not change over the centuries. Style and form change, but not the basic human emotions. Purists would have us believe that music from the so-called Classical period should be performed with emotional restraint, while so-called Romantic music should be played with emotional freedom. Such advice has often resulted in exaggeration: overindulgent, uncontrolled performances of Romantic music and dry, sterile dull performances of Classical music." He continued, "A dictionary definition of 'romantic' usually includes the following: 'Displaying or expressing love or strong affection; ardent, passionate, fervent.' I cannot name a single great composer of any period who did not possess these qualities. Isn't, then, *all* music romantic? And shouldn't the performer listen to his heart rather than to intellectual concepts of how to play Classical, Romantic or any other style of music?" While intellectual and technical elements are indeed present, music is ultimately the expression of the soul and should touch the hearts of those who hear it.

Summary of Artistic Devices

I. **Pitch**
   A. Vibrato
      1. Speed
      2. Width
   B. Glissando (slide)
   C. Ornaments (trills, mordents, etc.)

II. **Duration**
   A. Tempo (fast or slow)
   B. Staccato/Legato (short, detached notes/long, connected notes)
   C. Accelerando/Ritard (speed up/slow down)
   D. Fermata, Tenuto (holding certain notes longer than their written value)
   E. Rubato (changing the value of certain notes for a musical effect)
   F. Arpeggiating (rolling) a chord
   G. Inegale or double-dotting in Baroque music (exaggerating note values)

III. **Volume**
   A. Dynamics
      1. Contour (crescendo or decrescendo)
      2. Terrace (abrupt change from forte to piano or vice-versa)
   B. Accent (sfortzando)
   C. Balance between voices (bringing out melody, bass, or inner voices)

IV. **Tone**
   A. Right hand:
      1. Place where string is plucked (Ponticello–near bridge; Dolce–over soundhole)
      2. Angle of nail on string (Ponticello–center of nail; Dolce–side of nail)
      3. Direction of stroke (Ponticello–pull out from guitar; Dolce–"slice" string at angle towards left shoulder)
   B. Left hand
      1. Change position (Ponticello–lower positions; Dolce–upper positions)
      2. Add slur or slide
   C. Special Effects
      1. Harmonics
      2. Pizzicato
      3. Tambora
      4. Rasqueado
      5. Golpe

Part II

Repertoire

Repertoire

The next section of this book deals with repertoire of the classical guitar. It is divided by period of music with a brief description and includes performance notes on each piece. The pieces are not in graded order, but the list below ranks the pieces into three very general levels of ability (A is the easiest; C is the most difficult). It is the purpose of this section to acquaint the student with an overall view of the guitar repertoire while also refining technique and interpretation. The student can then use the knowledge gained from this book to pursue further repertoire in a similar manner.

The dates of each period are very general. Cultural developments advanced differently in each part of the world with a lot of overlapping and ambiguities in terms of style. There are also a number of smaller sub-periods or styles, such as French Impressionism (late 1800's to early 1900's). Music from the Modern period is not included here due to copyright restrictions, but there is a brief description of it along with a list of notable composers and suggested repertoire.

Choose pieces that appeal to you on the basis of your interest and technical ability. I suggest reading through all the performance notes because they contain ideas that might be applied to other compositions. These comments and suggestions are similar to those I would give a student in a private lesson. They represent only my viewpoint, and there are other ways to approach the music. The metronome settings and expression markings are editorial, as well.

I recommend listening to recordings of these pieces (see Appendix B) because I believe it is valuable to study a variety of interpretations. This is not to copy a particular one, but to expand our thinking in order to ultimately settle on our own individual style.

Renaissance Period
(1500–1625)

The Renaissance (literally *rebirth*) was a time of great revival and renewed interest in the arts. In fact, it was a period of rich development in many areas of life. Brilliant achievements were made in literature, architecture, science, and the arts. As a transition from the Middle Ages to modern times, the Renaissance ushered in an abundance of marvelous and fascinating music as well. Much of this was vocal, although there was also a considerable amount of polyphonic instrumental and dance music. Primary musical forms were dances (galliard, alman, pavane, etc.), fantasia, variations, and ricercars. Popular instruments included the lute, vihuela, and four-string guitar (Renaissance guitar), all of which provide a wealth of music that readily transcribes to the modern classical guitar from its original notation in tablature. All of the pieces presented in this section were originally written for one of these plucked string instruments.

Notable Composers: Besard, Byrd, Cutting, Dowland, Fuenllana, Galilei, Holborne, Johnson, LeRoy, Milan, Milano, Molinaro, Mudarra, Narvaez, Neusidler, Palestrina, Praetorious, Robinson and Valderrabano.

Performance Notes

Anonymous–*Danza* (p. 68)

Interpretation: The following four pieces are often performed as a set together with the *Preludio* (p. 52) and *Bianco Fiore* (p. 55). They are usually entitled *Six Lute Pieces of the Renaissance* and are performed in the order in which they appear in this book. This first piece contains two-measure phrases, with the exception of mm. 5–7 and mm. 8–10, which are three measures each. A loud/soft echo is very effective in these repeated phrases. Also create a contrast between the phrases at mm. 11–12 and mm. 13–14; they are parallel, although not identical.

Technique: Try a thumb strum at m. 11, either all flesh or all nail. If you use all nail, glide at a slight angle—do not play directly from the center of the thumbnail, as this will cause a thin or harsh sound. Use a 4th finger guide in mm. 5–6 and mm. 8–9. To avoid squeaks, lift the bass note fingers straight off the strings and then shift quickly.

Anonymous–*Gagliarda* (p. 69)

Interpretation: This bright dance, full of rhythmic variation, is clearly divided into four-measure sections. Strive for stark contrasts between ponticello and dolce, as marked. Be sure to give a slight accent on the first beat of each measure to maintain the three-beat feel. This is sometimes difficult because of the displaced bass notes in mm. 7, 15, and 23 that create an accent on the second beat of the measure. Try playing the repeated notes staccato in mm. 9, 13, and 21.

Technique: Practice with a metronome at first to help you define the rhythmic intent of the piece. Make sure to play the 16th note passages at mm. 9 and 21 in time. The harmonics at m. 8 will be clearer if plucked more towards the bridge with the thumbnail. Notice in m. 25 how the open 1st string aids in the transition from the upper 2nd string position to the lower position. Segovia would often use this technique to his technical and musical advantage.

Anonymous–*Canzone* (p. 70)

Interpretation: This melancholy piece should not be played too slowly. The first four measures serve as a stately introduction. Treat the sixteenth notes in m. 3 as an ornament—light and free.

Section two at m. 6 begins with a two-measure question and answer. M. 8 introduces a beautiful section of contrapuntal imitation. The five-note melodic motif begins in the mid-range bass voice and is imitated two beats later in the treble an octave higher. It is then introduced in the bass voice a fifth lower and again in the treble an octave higher, finally resolving on the A major chord in m. 10. Try to mimic your phrasing of the original motif in each imitation. The sequence then starts over again, but this time it begins in the higher octave and resolves to a surprise F major chord in m. 14. For tonal contrast, play the motif at m. 11 on the second string with a beautiful slow vibrato. Do the same for the identically fingered 4th string imitation that follows it.

Technique: Strive for proper dynamic balance of the opening chords. The melody should sing above the rest of the harmony. The run in m. 3 should be played free stroke, alternating *im* to maintain the delicate quality. In the imitation section, pay close attention to each voice, letting each note ring for its full value. The trill at the end of the piece should start as a pull-off from the A above. Start slowly and accelerate toward the end of the trill. Not only is this easier, but it also creates a nice musical effect.

This piece can be played in standard tuning as well, but it is fingered here with a low D so it may be performed with the other anonymous Renaissance lute pieces without interruption.

Anonymous–*Saltarello* (p. 70)

Interpretation: A quick Italian dance, the salterello has a light skipping quality. The one presented here is a wonderful finale to the collection of anonymous Italian lute pieces found in this book. Its melody is quite similar to the *volta* found in England during the same time period.

The most intriguing aspect of this work is the drone bass ostinato consistent throughout most of the piece. It provides a solid accompaniment but should not drown out the melody.

The piece contains sections of eight measures divided into four-measure phrases. This presents many opportunities for tone color and dynamic contrast. There are two main melodic themes in the piece with variations following each one. The first theme should float along lightly with effortless slurs. The second theme (starting at m. 17) is very effective played ponticello. The first theme is repeated at m. 33 an octave lower and should be played with a bright sound for extra clarity.

Technique: The most difficult aspect of the piece is coordinating the drone bass with the melody. It must be practiced quite slowly at first, paying close attention to the right-hand fingering to gain proper independence. This is one of the few pieces where practicing the melody alone would be beneficial since there are no fingered bass notes.

The long slurred runs also must be practiced separately to achieve evenness in both rhythm and volume. On these runs, try practicing to the end of the run, as if backing up from a finish line. For example, in m. 15, play the last two eighth notes and land firmly on the first beat of the next measure and stop there. When that move is perfected, back up and play

the last four eighth notes of m. 15, ending in the same spot. Perfect each segment before backing up to the next pair of eighth notes. Soon you will have backed up to the beginning of m. 13 and will have a very solid run. Be sure to use a properly balanced left-hand position with knuckles parallel to the neck. Pull down into the next string for strong slurs (like a rest stroke). Make sure they are even and strong, giving enough time to the first note of each pair.

Be sure to accent the highest note of the three ending harmonic chords.

Milan–*Pavane* (p. 72)

Interpretation: The pavane is a slow processional Italian court dance. Most pavanes are in quadruple meter (as is this one), although some are triple meter. This pavane comes from *El Maestro* (1535), a treatise on lute technique. The piece is divided into four-measure phrases, with the exception of the fourth group in which an extra measure is found. The contrapuntal fashion of this piece makes use of the *suspension*—a chord containing a non-harmonic note that is then resolved to a harmonic one. This series of tension/resolutions weaves through the entire piece, resolving solidly on the two half-note chords at the end of each four-bar phrase. Strive for a stately, regal (*maestoso*) performance with full-sounding chords.

Technique: Play this piece no faster than you can play the runs in mm. 18–19. Clock your speed there and then use it as your tempo. These runs should be practiced separately as little exercises. Use the exact same right-hand fingering each time for consistency and be sure to practice the runs back in context of the piece.

On the three and four-note chords—especially mm. 22–25—endeavor to bring out the highest voice, creating a pleasing balance. Accent the melody by using more force with the *a* finger, allowing the other fingers to play more passively. Proper balance in polyphonic music is difficult to achieve, but these chords should help you develop this skill.

On the tied suspensions (mm. 11, 14, 15, 16, 20) make sure to play the suspended note loud enough and hold it through the next chord so the harmonic suspension is maintained.

Johnson–*Alman* (p. 73)

Interpretation: The English alman (*allemande* in French) was a moderate dance in duple or quadruple meter. This one is composed of four sections of eight bars each. The second and fourth sections are variations of the first and third sections (AA'BB') and should be interpreted as such. When applying variation in dynamics and tone color, consider the piece in two-measure phrases. Be sure to start these phrases on the pick-up (fourth beat of previous measure). Note that the pick-up should not get the accent. It is a lead-in to the first beat of the measure, which should get the accent.

Observe that the general melodic shape is the same in both sections. Both lines start low, peak in the middle, and then descend again. In section A, the melody builds towards the high C in m. 3 and then works its way back down. In section B, a sequence begins in m. 17, leading to a peak at the end of m. 18. It then falls off in a sequence from that point all the way to m. 22 and finally to the end of the section. Keep this overall contour in mind when developing your two-measure phrases. Try increasing the volume toward the peaks of these contours and hold the highest notes slightly.

To add length to this piece, try repeating the first and last sections again at the end (AA'BB'AB').

Technique: Give particular rhythmic clarity to the dotted eighths in the opening section. To avoid lazy sixteenths, try setting the metronome click on every eighth note. Place the sixteenth notes exactly midway between each click. Contrast this articulation with a very legato variation of running eighth notes in the next section (A'). In the third and fourth sections (mm. 17–32) strive for a ringing effect, letting overtones ring as if you were hearing the echo of a lute played in an old church. Be sure to hold each note for its full value, as the overlapping of the contrapuntal lines is especially lovely. This is rather difficult at m. 19, but sustaining the high A is worth the stretch. Apply rest stroke to the A, as well as the other tied melody notes following, to accent the descending motion of the line.

Besard–*Branle and Volte* (p. 74)

Interpretation: This pair of dances contrasts nicely in feel. The *Branle* has a moderate 4/4 feel, while the *Volte* in a quick 3/4, is similar in feel to a jig. The *Branle* starts rather unusually on the 2nd beat of the measure, and all the two-measure phrases can be felt the same way—accent the 2nd beat of each of these phrases, giving a slight breath after the 1st beat before you start a new phrase. Notice also how mm. 3–4 are a variation of mm. 1–2 and mm. 7–8, a variation of 5–6. Mm. 9 and 10 are fingered in upper positions with the left hand to give a dolce tone. Use a thumb strum in the last measure to give more fullness to the final chord.

The *Volte* should have accents on the 1st, 3rd, and 5th eighth note of every measure to maintain a triple meter feel. However, there are a few spots where it may seem more appropriate to accent only the 1st and 4th eighth notes, giving the piece a 6/8 hemiola effect (mm. 6, 14). A *hemiola* is a displaced accent. Strive for quick strums to help keep the dance-like tempo and feel.

Technique: On the last beat of mm. 1 and 3 in the *Branle*, lift the chord and shift to the high B. If the stretch at m. 2 between the F# bass and the high A seems impossible, you can raise the last three bass notes of that measure up an octave. The jump in m. 7 to the F# is somewhat difficult but is worth the effort to achieve the beautiful 2nd string sound. Put the 2nd finger down as soon as possible after the 4th finger lands on the F#. In m. 9, the second open A bass aids in the transition to the 7th fret for the D and B. Make the shift as the bass note rings. Use 1st finger as a guide on the 3rd string down to the B.

In the *Volte*, set the 1st and 3rd fingers down in the pick-up measure and keep them there to form the D major chord at the beginning of the first measure. Accent the strums to achieve proper rhythmic feel. At m. 3, leave 3rd finger on G# while the 4th plays the high A. This will be an anchor as the 4th finger makes a quick change to the 2nd string E. At m. 4, let the high A ring slightly over the next two notes. The fast runs should be isolated and practiced separately. Pay special attention to right-hand fingering on these as well. Be sure not to let bass notes ring through when there is a change in harmony, as in m. 14—dampen the A with the back of the thumb as you play the D.

Dowland–*Galliard* (p. 75)

Interpretation: The galliard is a lively dance of Italian origin, usually in triple meter. The one that appears here is neither Italian nor in triple meter. Rather, it is attributed to the foremost English lutenist of the Elizabethan Era, John Dowland, and is written in simple duple meter (2/4). Although credited to Dowland, this piece may actually be the work of Mexican composer Manuel Ponce, who wrote many pieces for Segovia in the style of other composers.

This selection has a straight-forward simplicity. Strive for a bright march-like feel with a brisk tempo. I recorded this piece on *Pleasures of Their Company* using a capo on the third fret to match the original lute tuning. To lengthen this piece, it was recorded AABBAAB.

Technique: Use more center of the nail to achieve the lute-like nasal quality. Play predominantly in the ponticello position. In mm. 11 and 18, use rest stroke on the high A and dampen bass strings from ringing as you play it. Experiment with rolling chords. You may find it desirable to roll only the first and last chords of the piece in order to keep a bright staccato feel. The last chord can be rolled using the thumb on the two bass strings and then the fingers on the trebles.

Dowland—*Allemande* (p. 76)

Interpretation: Also recorded on *Pleasures of Their Company* (capo third fret), this piece is one of the most famous of Dowland's works. Strive for a bright dance-like feel with much dynamic and tonal contrast between phrases. For example, the first two measures can be played loud ponticello, and the repeating mm. 3–4 can be played soft dolce. Both should have a slightly staccato feel. Notice mm. 9–16 are an embellishment of mm. 1–8. Your interpretation can reflect this. Give a break between phrases by stopping all notes fully before starting a new phrase. Strive for full sonorous chords at mm. 23–26. Also contrast mm. 31–34 with 35–36. Crescendo the passage starting on

the last beat of m. 38 up to the peak at the high A in m. 40.

Technique: Pay close attention to even the smallest details to help bring out the full musical essence of this piece. Observe all fingerings, hold all notes the proper length, and make sure you understand all the rhythms.

For the brightest, most powerful sound in the opening two measures, play near the bridge, on the center of the nail, and pluck the string outward from the face of the guitar using a stiffened hand and fingers. Also use the weight of your forearm for full power in the chords at mm. 23–26. The third chord is notated as a thumb strum. Flatten your left hand 4th finger slightly to dampen the 5th string as you strum. In the following passage at mm. 27–28, your 4th finger can act as a pivot as you change between chords. At m. 29, be sure to let each melody note ring to the next, achieving a unique harmonic effect. This same effect occurs at m. 41.

DANZA

See Notes, p. 65

ANONYMOUS

GAGLIARDA

See Notes, p. 65

ANONYMOUS

CANZONE

See Notes, p. 65

ANONYMOUS

SALTARELLO

See Notes, p. 66

ANONYMOUS

PAVANE

See Notes, p. 66

Luis Milan

*Alternate for ms. 13:

ALMAN

See notes, p. 66

Robert Johnson

BRANLE

See notes, p. 67

JEAN-BAPTISTE BESARD

VOLTE

See notes, p. 67

JEAN-BAPTISTE BESARD

GALLIARD

See notes, p. 67

John Dowland

ALLEMANDE

See notes, p. 68

JOHN DOWLAND

Baroque Period
(1625–1750)

Roughly coinciding with the lifetime of its greatest composer J.S. Bach, the Baroque period saw great strides in the development of vocal and instrumental music. The music was highly ornate, often improvised, and full of dynamic tension. The present major/minor system of tonality was developed along with the even-tempered (well-tempered) tuning system we use today. Many composers were supported by either the church or elite wealthy patrons. Important musical forms include the concerto grosso, sonata, variations, fugue, chorale, cantata, oratorio, and aria. Another major form was the suite which contained some or all of the following movements: prelude, allemande, courante, sarabande, optional dances (minuet, gavotte, bourrée) and gigue. Compositional devices such as homophonic and contrapuntal textures, abrupt changes in dynamics, strong rhythmic drive, and singular melodic ideas characterized music of this period. Keyboard works as well as solo violin, cello, lute, and baroque guitar music are the basis of present day transcriptions for guitar.

Notable Composers: Albinoni, Bach, Batchelar, Campion, Corbetta, Corelli, Couperin, de Murcia, de Visée, Gaultier, Frescobaldi, Froberger, Handel, Logy, Lully, Monteverdi, Purcell, Rameau, Roncalli, Sanz, Scarlatti, Telemann, Vivaldi, Weiss.

Performance Notes

de Visée–*Prelude and Bourrée* (p. 80)

Interpretation: This *Prelude* and *Bourrée* are from the *Suite in D Minor*. The *Prelude* should have a rather free interpretation, taking time between phrases. These phrases, for the most part, begin on the second eighth note of each measure. Notice the question and answer phrases at m. 5. A four-note melodic motif begins on the second eighth note of the measure and is then answered by the next four eighth notes. The same thing occurs in mm. 6 and 7. Bring out this dialogue by shaping these motifs dynamically and rhythmically.

Strive for a moderate dance-like tempo and feel in the *Bourrée*. Consider using a slight accent on the 1st beat of mm. 1–3 and 5–7. Also accent the descending bass line in mm. 9–11 and crescendo towards the peak on the 3rd beat of m. 11. Pause slightly and add vibrato to the high note on the 1st beat of m. 13 before falling off into the run.

Technique: The opening of the *Prelude* is fingered on the second string because of its warm sound and the ability to add more vibrato. The mordent in m. 8 should be played F–E–F–E. The second finger on F from the previous beat sets up this fingering. The trill in m. 9 should start on the upper note (D–C#–D–C#, etc.) and should accelerate slightly towards the end of the trill. Alternate between the 2nd and 3rd fingers for more control and speed.

The *Bourrée* should not present much difficulty. At m. 3, pull slurs downward into next string (like a rest stroke) for evenness. Notice the unusual fingering of m. 11 where the 4th finger on F# becomes a guide to G and then acts as a pivot in the next chord change. The Gm chord on the second beat of the measure can be fingered as a bar chord instead, if desired. The following measure does contain a full bar Gm chord and should be strummed with an all flesh thumb.

On the 3rd beat of m. 15 at the final cadence, use a vertical vibrato (motion parallel to the fret) on the second string D. To create the illusion of a crescendo on that note, delay the vibrato slightly, then do it slow and wide in pitch. Two or three bends of the string both up and down should be sufficient.

Sanz–*Pavanas* (p. 81)

Interpretation: The intrigue of this ancient Spanish dance lies in its interweaving of contrapuntal lines. The moving line shifts frequently between bass and treble voices. Highlight this motion to give the piece direction, but be sure to let the stationary voices ring for their full value to achieve the contrapuntal effect.

For the most part, the phrases in this piece start in the middle of the measure and are usually two measures in length. Unlike many pieces, there is no repetition of thematic material—the piece moves through various similar melodic ideas. This textural variety provides the opportunity to bring out phrases with added tone color and dynamic contrast.

Technique: Rest stroke should be limited in this piece to a few isolated accented notes. Free stroke on the melody will give a more legato sound and will better match the sound of the thumb when it takes over the moving voice.

The slide at m. 24 facilitates the large shift from the 3rd position to the 7th fret. On the wide stretches at mm. 18, 22, and 24, be sure to relax the left hand before the reach.

For the unique group of slurs at mm. 28–29, be sure to hammer-on with a good deal of force and especially accent the highest note with the use of vibrato. The long slur from the open string will be clearer with a certain brightness, so play the phrase ponticello, as marked.

Bach–*Bourrée* (p. 82)

Interpretation: This piece is a fine example of two-voice *counterpoint*. Literally, this means point against point (line against line). In other words, there are two separate and distinct voices moving throughout the entire piece. In fact, this piece is presented as a duet in Volume One of this method. It is helpful to play each line (bass and treble) separately to hear how each moves by itself. Then be aware of the movement of each voice when playing them together, highlighting the interesting motion. The treble line will generally take precedence, except in phrases where the bass line is featured, such as mm. 4, 12, 16, and 20. Do not let the bass line overshadow the melody throughout the piece. Just bring it out occasionally for effect.

Technique: All three mordents begin on the upper note. The only one notated in Bach's original was at m. 15. However, it was so often customary to perform them at cadences (mm. 7 and 23) that they are included here. A *cadence* is a chord progression at the end of a phrase or section that gives the impression of momentary or permanent conclusion.

Start the piece slowly enough to be able to get through the last four measures at tempo. These should be practiced separately, as both the treble and bass lines are quite active at this point. Notice the fingering of the bass line in m. 16. The D#, played on the 5th string, sets up the end of the phrase. To avoid a squeak, jump to the D#—do not slide your first finger to the note. Slurs may be added to some of the eighth notes, if desired.

Bach–*Prelude* (p. 83)

Interpretation: Keep the tempo to produce the full dramatic impact of this piece. Embellish the piece with frequent changes of tone color and dynamic contrast. Certain slurs should be used for accents (such as the high A in m. 9) and others for a legato, flowing feel (such as the opening measure). The latter should not be overly accented.

Start the piece with a relaxed feel and let the piece build in intensity until the end. The piece takes a momentary break in the middle at m. 22. Ritard slightly before the strummed chord and pause briefly on it. Then start building again. Pay special attention to the build-up starting at m. 31, peaking on the high A in m. 34 and then diminishing until the final and most intense build-up from mm. 37 to 39. Once reaching a dynamic peak at m. 39, maintain the volume and intensity until the end of the piece. Ritard on the last part of m. 41.

Technique: Strive for even slurs, unless an accent is desired. The slide in m. 5 facilitates left-hand fingering and sounds almost identical to a slur in this situation. In runs on the bass strings, such as in mm. 19 and 28, try playing right-hand fingers more on the center of the nail to avoid the sound of the nail swiping across the wound bass strings, creating a scraping sound. The thumb can also be used, but try to match the sound of the fingers that start the runs. The chords below the pull-offs in mm. 24 and 26 should actually be held for an eighth note—through the end of the slur.

For the long pedal tone passage starting in m. 33, strive for a full, round sound with the thumb on the 3rd and 4th strings. Try slicing the string from the left side of the thumbnail riding toward the center. (See explanation of thumb technique in Appendix A.) Some prefer playing the thumb rest stroke. Listen to Segovia's recording of this piece to hear the beautiful full round sound he gets here. At the end of m. 35, I suggest gradually moving toward a ponticello sound, returning to dolce at the end of m. 36. In mm. 37 and 38, lock the *i* and *a* fingers together and play from the wrist on the ascending two-note chords. Use rest stroke on the high D's and C#'s in mm. 39–41.

Scarlatti–*Sonata in A* (p. 86)

Interpretation: This piece is a two-part (treble and bass) contrapuntal sonata. Maintain a solid rhythmic feel, allowing each voice to ring for its full value. Vary the articulation of the melody to achieve a bright, dance-like feel. Sometimes play staccato, other times legato. For example, repeated notes (such as in mm. 15, 23, 25, etc.) sound slightly better played staccato. The addition of slurs also creates variety in the articulation of the notes.

Try to bring out the dialogue between phrases, such as between mm. 7–8 and mm. 9–10. These phrases actually start on the pick-up from the measures preceding them. Allow the second phrase (mm. 9–10) to "answer" the first. The piece is filled with complimentary phrases such as these.

Scarlatti makes use of the *apoggiatura* (literally *leaning*) frequently in this piece. Notice the first two beats of mm. 16, 17, 18, 30, and 32. Each of these has a dissonant first note that strongly resolves on the second beat. The first note "leans" into the second. Linger on the dissonant note slightly for more emphasis (this will occur naturally, as well, because it is the downbeat of the measure).

Technique: The grace notes at mm. 24 and 62 are difficult and may require some isolated practice. They should be crisp and precise, not distracting from the rhythmic clarity of the line. The one in m. 24 is easier if you leave the 2nd finger planted on G coming into the measure. The mordents in this piece are slurred up to the next note in the scale and then back to the starting note. For example, in m. 8, play D–E–D.

The thumb strums at mm. 19–20 are added for intensity and tonal variety. Try an all pad sound. The slide at m. 64 is another artistic device, allowing for the warmer sounding higher position fingering of the passage. The slides at mm. 36, 40, 74, and 78 facilitate left-hand fingering and are virtually indistinguishable from slurs.

Notice the unusual cross-string slur at m. 41. Strike the G# and then hammer-on the F# on the next string. The 4th string should still be ringing from the previous D#, but the string now changes function from accompaniment to melody. Segovia would often use cross-string slurs to create a more legato line. Many times he would slur to a string that had not been plucked at all by the right hand.

I play the notes as they are written, but it is God who makes the music.

–Johann Sebastian Bach

PRELUDE

See Notes, p. 77

Robert de Visée

BOURRÉE

See Notes, p. 77

Robert de Visée

PAVANAS

See Notes, p. 77

GASPAR SANZ

BOURRÉE
(from 1st Lute Suite)

See Notes, p. 78

JOHANN SEBASTIAN BACH

PRELUDE
(from 1st Cello Suite)

See Notes, p. 78

JOHANN SEBASTIAN BACH

SONATA IN A
(L. 483)

See Notes, p. 78

Domenico Scarlatti

Classical Period
(1750–1850)

The most important period for the history and development of the guitar, the Classical period saw the advent of our modern instrument. Classical music in general was being accepted by the masses, and composers responded to this new audience. Compositional practice tended towards structure with simplicity, formalism with elegance, and correctness of style and form. The symphony orchestra was born, and main musical forms included the symphony, sonata, sonatina, string quartet, and theme and variations. Textures were primarily homophonic—a single melodic idea with accompaniment. Melodic phrases were short and clearly defined. Virtuoso guitarist/composers left a heritage of outstanding concert works, didactic studies, and even concertos for guitar and chamber orchestra. The earliest guitar method books were published during this era, giving insight to the teaching and philosophies of the patriarchs of the classical guitar.

Notable Composers: Beethoven, Haydn, Mozart. *For guitar:* Aguado, Carcassi, Carulli, Coste, Diabelli, Giuliani, Legnani, Mertz, Molino, Paganini, Sor.

Performance Notes

Carcassi–*Study in E Minor* (p. 94)

Interpretation: This piece is divided into four main sections of eight measures each, with the exception of the last section, which is twelve measures. Each section can be divided into four-measure and then again into two-measure phrases. Keep this in mind when planning tonal contrast. You may wish to sing the melody to decide how you want to interpret the contour of these phrases. Also try playing just the melody and bass, leaving out the two inner voices. Compare this piece with Carcassi's *Study in A*. Notice the similarities in motion. For example, mm. 17–20 has a static melody line, causing suspense, and the bass line moves up by half-step, increasing tension. This finally resolves on the high B chord in m. 24. Ritard at this climax on the bass notes leading into the recapitulation in m. 25.

Measure 28 contains a surprise harmony that the composer exploits in the next four measures—a brief key change (*modulation*) that eventually makes its way back to end the piece in its original key. Mm. 29–32 are actually an added insert, accounting for the extra length of this section. Highlight the repeated two-measure phrase by using a dolce sound on the first and ponticello on the other to create an echo effect.

Technique: Use rest stroke on the melody. A metronome is useful for playing in time, especially since it can be hard to follow the beat where the two inner voices are repeated over and over (mm. 2, 4, etc.). The metronome will also help build speed. Start at a moderate tempo and gradually increase it until you can play the piece accurately at the desired speed. Once you have achieved your goal, discontinue the use of the metronome to concentrate on the freedom of

expression in regard to rhythm and tempo.

Transitions between chords can be aided by playing the bass note slightly ahead of the melody note (arpeggiating the chord). This creates a nice musical effect, but you would not want to use it on every chord.

Measure 21 is marked as a partial bar (⅚I) where the 1st finger pivots on the bass note from the measure before to form the bar. If you find that some of the notes pressed by the bar finger are not clear, you may wish to use a full bar. You may also adjust the finger up or down as necessary, depending on what is easiest for you personally. For a smooth transition to the full bars in mm. 24 and 35, form the bar and then add the other fingers as you need them.

Carcassi–*Study in A* (p. 95)

Interpretation: This is one of Carcassi's most melodic compositions and a favorite among guitarists. Clearly divided into four-measure phrases, this piece makes full use of the guitar's polyphonic capabilities by maintaining four voices throughout: melody, bass, and two inner voices. The main concept of the piece can be grasped by playing it through with only the bass and melody voices. For the most part, the bass notes fall on beats 1 and 4, and the melody on beats 2 and 3. The middle voices are added for texture and atmosphere, and it is also interesting to play these alone as two-note chords (mostly thirds) to observe their movement and smooth voice leading.

Notice the step-wise motion of the bass and melody. They often move by half-step, creating tension, drive or intensity. A static voice creates suspense, such as the low E pedal in mm. 9–12. An abrupt change in harmony (mm. 6, 13, 16, 21, and 23) or sudden change in rhythm or texture (mm. 7, 16) will also indicate some type of musical significance.

To best understand the interpretation of this piece, here is a brief discussion of the more important aspects phrase by phrase:

mm. 1–4   Opening theme: peaks in last measure but also comes full circle back to the tonic A chord, creating a sense of completeness.

5–8   Bass builds by half-step and harmony ends on dominant chord, generating a sense of expectation.

9–12   Low E bass pedal is static, creating suspense.

13–16   Bass moves by half-step, producing tension. The treble then takes over the half-step motion to build to the highest climax of the piece in m. 16 on the C# major chord. The non-triplet eighth notes at m. 16 are a nice transition back to a repeat of the opening measure.

17–20   This section is very similar to the opening theme, this time with a suspenseful static A bass pedal.

21–24   Abrupt change of harmony precedes peak at m. 22, which highlights the D on the 4th beat. Another sudden change of harmony and texture creates final tension before resolving back on the last A chord.

By analyzing a piece in this fashion, you can start to develop interpretive ideas. In general, give extra emphasis to the moving lines. Contour your dynamics to follow the phrases, adding tone color, rubato, vibrato, and terrace dynamics for variation.

Technique: Use rest strokes on the melody notes to bring them out above the accompaniment. Try a pad rest stroke thumb on mm. 9 and 10 for a dolce sound, then switch to a ponticello free stroke thumb at mm. 11 and 12.

Measure 16 contains two triplets and four non-triplet eighth notes. Play this passage in time first to get the feel of moving from three notes per beat to two. Later, add the ritard, making sure to keep the *two against three* feel. Avoid sounding the eighth notes as quarter notes. These notes are fingered all on the 4th string to give them a cello-like quality. Play very legato and use ample vibrato to help control intonation.

On the fermata at m. 22, stop the bass note from ringing, dampen any unwanted noise, and add vibrato. The next two notes are almost an afterthought and can even be omitted, if desired.

When changing chords in this piece, set down only what you need first and then add the other notes from there. This will keep the music moving smoothly. Also use guide and anchor fingers whenever possible (such as the last C# in the first measure to the D in the next).

Carcassi–*Study in A Minor* (p. 96)

Interpretation: This brilliant study should be played fast enough to achieve the illusion of a sustained note in the tremolo measures. Vary the speed, however, to make the sixteenth notes more interesting. There should be a natural "ebb and flow," or give and take, to the rhythm and dynamics. Some of the measures have two voices and some have three. In certain places you will want to bring out the bass line (most of the piece), but in others, the treble line should stand out (especially mm. 13–16, part of 17, etc.). Generally, you will want to highlight the moving voice. When both voices move, the highest one usually takes precedence, as in mm. 13–14. This phrase is a perfect example of contrary motion between voices. When the bass descends, the melody ascends, and vice-versa. Each voice continues in the same direction for three beats then reverses on the fourth beat in each measure. Crescendo towards the third beat, then drop back down on four and start again.

Contour dynamics should be used primarily in this piece. Follow the melodic lines and shape your dynamics accordingly. Use *terrace* dynamics in the parallel passages of mm. 16–17 (loud) and mm. 18–19 (soft) for a nice echo effect. You can even use contour dynamics in each of these phrases, peaking on the high B.

Give a slight break between phrases—a breath, so to speak. After the first four measures the piece starts over again, so taper the end of the first phrase with a slight ritard and decrescendo. Start the new phrase again with about the same intensity as the opening measure. In m. 20 the line changes direction midway through the measure. This is a good place to start the ritard, actually pausing slightly on the 3rd beat E. This sets up the recapitulation of the theme in the following measure. The last measure of the piece should have a ritard to avoid an abrupt finish.

Technique: The main difficulty of this piece is in achieving a consistent "rapid-fire" succession of notes. Practice in small bursts of speed, working on only one beat at a time. Always practice to the bass note of the next beat. This will give you a strong place to land (the thumb stroke) and also allows you to overlap each beat. Expand this to practicing one measure at a time, again playing to the downbeat of the next measure. In addition, it is wise to practice the whole piece slowly and accurately, gradually increasing the tempo to the desired speed. Practice particularly difficult sections separately, as well (mm. 8, 16–17, etc.).

To work out left-hand changes, try playing each beat as a chord, combining the two or three notes. Playing through the piece this way will not only help in solidifying left-hand moves without the distraction of the right hand, but will also give you a chance to hear the remarkable voice-leading of the lines together.

You may wish to use the alternate *pimi* to finger the tremolo patterns in the first measure and others like it. This might help maintain consistency with the arpeggio measures with which the tremolo measures alternate.

Follow right-hand fingering carefully in m. 8. Accent F and A by using rest stroke. Dampen all bass strings with the thumb as you play the high A to obtain a clean stop. Also use rest stroke on the slurred notes in the pedal point runs at mm. 16–19 to bring out the ascending line. The open E's can be played free stroke.

The "ebb and flow" interpretation should allow for minute technical breaks. Relax the right hand as much as possible throughout, but especially at these rest stops and let-ups provided by rubato, tenuto, ritards, etc. One such spot is the difficult change to the chord at the first beat of m. 23. I suggest jumping to the bass note D and pausing slightly to set the other notes in place. This not only aids technically, but creates a wonderful musical effect, especially if you add vibrato to the D. Segovia would often transform a technical difficulty such as this into a musical advantage.

Sor–*Study in A* (p. 97)

Interpretation: This short etude was chosen for its simplicity and beauty. It contains a homogeneous texture of eight notes throughout, although the melody notes should ring for a quarter note each. Every melody note is followed by a two-note chord on the offbeat. These chords should be played staccato and more quietly than the melody notes for proper balance. The piece is divided into two-measure phrases, starting and ending in the middle of the measure. Shape your phrases to follow the rise and fall of the melodic contour. Contrast the similar phrases at mm. 8–10 and 10–12 with a change in dynamics and/or tone color. Pause on the beautiful surprise E# at m. 14, as well as the peak B in that measure and in the following one. Ritard at the end of each section, especially at the end of the piece, since it ends in the middle of the measure on the eighth note of a weak 2nd beat. Normally pieces end on strong beats such as the downbeat (first beat) or 3rd beat.

Technique: Use rest stroke on melody for fullness of sound and to help dampen the previous two-note chord. Also lift left-hand fingers off cleanly to stop the chord from ringing. It should be stopped exactly as the next melody note is played. You will also have to set the right thumb down to stop any open bass strings and any other notes that cannot be dampened by either the rest stroke or left-hand lift. At m. 7 the 4th finger is a guide into m. 8. This may create a slight portamento, if you wish. The second string fingering gives a more beautiful sound and also allows for

vibrato. M. 14 is fingered in the 5th position for the same reason.

Sor–*Study in B Minor* (p. 98)

Interpretation: Perhaps the most famous of all the Sor studies, this lovely etude has an elegant simplicity that accounts for its charm. The melody should always sing out above the accompaniment, and again I suggest singing or playing the melody by itself to fully grasp its character. The piece is formed in eight-measure sections—let the piece breathe naturally by feeling these phrases.

Bring out moving lines. At m. 25, vibrato the D#, as it is a nice source of tension until it resolves to the E in m. 26. Mm. 27–28 contain an almost parallel phrase. M. 29 starts as if it were going to be parallel as well, but it takes a surprise turn. Highlight the harmonic motion in this section with a change of tone color on one or more of the two-measure phrases. A subtle and gradual change to ponticello in mm. 29–31 would be effective before the dolce m. 32. The final section of the piece starts building from m. 41 to the peak at m. 44. Crescendo and accelerate slightly to the peak, then feature the second high B by adding vibrato while stopping all the other strings from ringing. A ritard and decrescendo would be appropriate for the end of the piece.

Technique: Use rest stroke on the melody, except perhaps where you desire a ponticello sound. For smoother transitions, use guide fingers such as the 1st finger between mm. 11–12 and the 2nd finger between 27–28 and 31–32.

In the series of bar chords at mm. 40–42, ride along the neck with the bottom of the index finger as you make a transition from one position to the next. Alternatively, you could use a hinge bar at m. 41 and then proceed into the next bar chord riding along the index finger.

This piece makes an excellent exercise for analyzing chord inversions for the key of B minor. Observing the harmonic content can also aid in memorization.

Sor–*Minuet in C* (p. 99)

Interpretation: The last movement of the *Grand Sonata*, Op. 25, this is one of the most popular of the Sor minuets. The writing is very classical in nature, almost imitating a string quartet. The minuet is a dance that originated in the Baroque period and is quite rhythmic. The theme of this piece is light and tuneful, typical of the classical period.

The repeats in this piece need not be observed literally. Playing straight through with the *D.C. al Fine* would be sufficient. Use a variety of tone color to help define the different sections of the piece. M. 29 starts a unique sequence where the melody with grace notes somewhat imitates a violin, and the two accompaniment notes, a viola and cello. These notes can be played slightly staccato, like the viola and cello playing pizzicato. At m. 37, the cello takes the melody, with the violin and viola providing accompaniment. Additional interpretive ideas are marked in the score. Notice the contrasting fingering of runs at mm. 44–45 and 60–61. Also unusual are the thumb strums of mm. 56–58.

Technique: Keep the 1st finger on C in m. 1 before starting the turn on beat 3. This measure may need to be practiced separately for an even, strong slur. Be sure to "pluck" downward and into the adjacent string with the left-hand fingers throughout the piece.

To achieve staccato chords in mm. 29–36, set your right-hand fingers back on the strings after playing them. Try rest stroke on the 1st beat of each measure.

Use a full strum with the pad of the thumb at m. 44. Alternate fingers on the next run for fluidity. The strum at m. 56 should be light, so as not to override the turn. Use a pad strum on the bass notes in the following two measures.

Sor–*Waltz in E* (p. 101)

Interpretation: This delightful waltz contains a number of wonderful special effects and gives much possibility for tonal and dynamic contrast. It also contains quite a bit of rhythmic variety, adding to its intrigue. The first two sections of this piece are in E major and the next two sections are in the parallel minor key (E minor). The piece then repeats the first two sections (*D.C. al Fine*).

In the first section, try this articulation of the repeated melody notes: In m. 1, play the E's on beats two and three slightly staccato, then let the next E (on the first beat of m. 2) ring longer, like an appoggiatura, before it resolves to the D#. Repeat this articulation in mm. 3–4 and 5–6. Be sure to crescendo the ascending 3rds at mm. 9, 13, and 27. Try contrasting mm. 17–20 with 21–24, maybe playing the second group softer. Strive for trumpet-like ponticello octaves at mm. 24 and 28. Play the dolce violin-like 3rds at mm. 26–28 very warmly. An alternative to this interpretation is to stay ponticello for the 3rds in mm. 26–28 and then to play the next set of octave B's dolce on the 2nd and 4th strings. The pizzicato octaves at m. 30 should be staccato and accented. The slur and harmonic section starting at m. 33 should feel light and graceful. Notice the slide at m. 39 for a change of color. After the *da capo* repeat, you could possibly end the piece with a full E chord strum

at m. 16 (EBEG#BE). Play it softly and short with a pad thumb.

Technique: Be sure to play the 32nd notes at m. 5 fast enough so as to contrast them with the triplets in mm. 1 and 3. Practice m. 6 first without the grace note to get the correct rhythm. Then add the grace note, keeping the same feel. On the pull-offs at mm. 9, 13, and 27, try not to hit the first string with the left-hand finger pulling off. The melody is on the first string, and each note should ring for a full beat. *M. 14 was fingered by Sor himself.* Notice that the switching of voices on the strings makes a smoother transition between chords.

To achieve the brightest sound on the octaves at mm. 24–26 and 28–30, stiffen your fingers and play more on the center of the nail near the bridge. Use the power of your whole hand to pluck out slightly from the face of the guitar. Use the left side of the nail with your fingers locked together, and pluck towards the left shoulder on the thirds at mm. 26–28 for a contrasting dolce sound. Pinch the pizzicato octaves together, laying the side of your hand on the strings near the bridge to muffle the strings.

The turns at mm. 33–38 need to be crisp and clear. Set all three fingers on the string as soon as possible, and keep the left hand parallel to the neck. Notice the difference in the slur patterns between mm. 33–34 and mm. 37–38 for added contrast. Make sure to touch the harmonics directly over the fret. It is a quick jump up, so look ahead as you are playing the open string chord preceding it.

Giuliani–*Rondo* (p. 102)

Interpretation: A *rondo* is a piece that always returns to the main theme. True to form, this piece is structured ABACA. Notice how the mood of this piece changes as it modulates from the haunting melody in E minor of section A to the contrasting themes of the more joyful relative and parallel major keys (G and E) in sections B and C. Also contrasting are the textures used in this piece. Section A contains an arpeggio accompaniment, while the other two sections are a study in 3rds and 6ths against a pedal bass. Observe the rise and fall of the melody in all sections by shaping your phrases with dynamics and rubato. Accent the 6ths in mm. 10 and 11 to "answer" the melodic "question" of the 3rds surrounding them.

Technique: Use *p* on the 6th and 3rd strings in section A (four times per measure) to give the bass line a steady rhythm. In sections B and C, lock right-hand fingers together to play the 3rds (*im*) and 6ths (*ia*). Play from the wrist and forearm, using the full weight of the hand to achieve more power. Be sure not to play the open bass string pedal too loudly. You may wish to practice m. 4 first without the grace note to get the correct rhythm. The double slurs of mm. 8 and 12 help achieve fluidity in the line of melodic 3rds.

Giuliani–*Theme and Variations* (p. 103)

Interpretation: This piece is the first movement of the Sonatina, Op. 71, No. 1. Like many theme and variations of the classical period, the theme and each of its variations are divided into two sections of eight measures each. The variations in this set are rhythmic in nature. The theme is stated in quarter notes, the 1st variation in 8th notes, the 2nd variation in triplets, and the final variation in 16th notes. This increasing subdivision of the beat creates a natural acceleration toward the final chords, giving the piece direction and drive. Be sure not to start the theme too fast, so you can maintain the tempo through the end of the piece. Keep a steady tempo to highlight the natural rhythmic variations. Unlike many pieces of this nature, the variations stay quite close to the original theme in melodic and harmonic content. Use variation in tonal and dynamic contrast to create interest.

Technique: This piece is excellent for sightreading practice, and since it stays in first position, editorial fingerings are minimal. Practice with a metronome initially to keep the tempo and to hear the gradual increase of intensity of the 8ths, triplets, and 16ths.

At m. 27, form a bar on the fourth 8th note of the measure to help get to the following F bass. Lift the bottom of the bar momentarily for the open B and then replace it to dampen the B while you play the A. On the ascending arpeggios (mm. 33–34, 55, etc.), you can plant or prepare your right-hand fingers by setting them on the strings at the beginning of each pattern, if you wish. The runs at mm. 52 and 60 may need to be isolated to practice separately and then put back in context of the piece.

Giuliani–*Allegro Spiritoso* (p. 105)

Interpretation: This piece is a miniature example of some of the great works of the classical period and contains many of the compositional devices used in Giuliani's larger concert selections. Like some of Sor's works, you can envision this piece being played by a small string ensemble and interpret it as such. The four-bar phrases usually begin on the pick-up note(s), so keep this in mind when developing tone color and dynamic contrast. Start your contrast on the pick-up and end it before the next pick-up.

The chords in m. 2 and the bass notes in the complimentary m. 4 sound good slightly staccato. In mm. 11 and 15, crescendo to the peak of the phrase and then come down to the chord in the following measure. Mm. 17 and 21 start phrases that are similar to each other. Try playing the first one loudly and then start the second phrase softly, making a crescendo on the 3rds in m. 22. Note the repeated passage of mm. 24–25 at mm. 26–27. Try terrace dynamics (loud/soft) for a nice echo effect. Resume a forte volume at m. 28 to complete the phrase. Crescendo through mm. 30 and 31, with a sudden decrease in volume on the chord at m. 32. Again crescendo m. 33 to the first beat of m. 34, where you should decrescendo the phrase all the way to the beginning of m. 36. Crescendo from the end chords at m. 44 to the high D at m. 46.

Technique: The slurs need to be even in sound and rhythm. Be sure to hammer-on with sufficient force to help equalize the volume. The broken thirds sections (mm. 22, 30–35) can be isolated and practiced as two-note chords, rather than broken ones, in order to solidify left-hand changes. They should be played p-i. In m. 17, keep the 2nd finger on D the whole measure to act as an anchor for the slurs.

Be sure to observe the rests in this piece. Stop the string(s) from ringing completely. This, along with the staccato passages and dynamic contrast, will serve to emulate the sound of a string ensemble.

Music must never offend the ear; it must please the hearer. In other words, it must never cease to be music.

–Wolfgang Amadeus Mozart

STUDY IN E MINOR

(Op. 60, No. 19)

See Notes, p. 89

MATTEO CARCASSI

STUDY IN A
(Op. 60, No. 3)

See Notes, p. 89

MATTEO CARCASSI

STUDY IN A MINOR
(Op. 60, No. 7)

See Notes, p. 90

Matteo Carcassi

STUDY IN A
(Op. 6, No. 2)

See Notes, p. 91

FERNANDO SOR

STUDY IN B MINOR
(Op. 35, No. 22)

See Notes, p. 91

FERNANDO SOR

MINUET IN C
(Op. 25)

See Notes, p. 91

FERNANDO SOR

WALTZ IN E
(Op. 32, No. 2)

See Notes, p. 92

FERNANDO SOR

D.C. al Fine

RONDO

See Notes, p. 92

MAURO GIULIANI

THEME AND VARIATIONS
(Op. 71, No. 1)

See Notes, p. 93

MAURO GIULIANI

ALLEGRO SPIRITOSO
(Op. 1, No. 10)

See Notes, p. 93

Mauro Giuliani

Romantic Period
(1850–1910)

Often called the "Golden Age" of concert music, the Romantic period is responsible for much of the serious music heard in concert halls today. As audiences grew, composers desired bigger sounds, expanded instrumentation, and more freedom of expression. They exploited melodic and harmonic contrast with frequent changes in tempo and meter. Freedom of form and tonal contrast also contributed to the emotional expression of this period. Although composers did still use some of the classical forms such as the sonata, sonatina, symphony, and studies, miniature character pieces were created to produce an intense emotional response as well. This type of piece works quite beautifully on the guitar with its intimate nature and variety of tonal colors, and some are included in this section.

Notable Composers: Albéniz, Berlioz, Bizet, Brahms, Chopin, Dvorak, Elgar, Falla, Franck, Granados, Grieg, Liszt, Mahler, Mendelssohn, Moussorgsky, Puccini, Offenbach, Rimsky-Korsakov, Saint-Saëns, Schubert, Schumann, Sibelius, Strauss, Tchaikovsky, Wagner, and Weber. *For guitar:* Barrios, Fortea, Mertz, Pujol, Tárrega.

French Impressionistic: Debussy, Poulenc, Ravel, Satie.

Performance Notes

Tárrega—*Estudio* (p. 111)

Interpretation: Although lesser known than many of Tárrega's works, this charming little study is quite easy to learn. The melody falls on the 2nd, 3rd, and 4th beats of each measure, while the bass is always on the first beat. By playing just the bass and melody alone, you can observe the main shape of the piece. The two middle voices are added to create the flowing triplet arpeggio, which makes a nice setting for the simple melody line. The harmonic content is very tonal, staying in the key of C major and its related chords. When the harmony does move to a borrowed chord, such as in mm. 5, 7, and 11, try to vary tone color or volume to feature the change. Also highlight the melodic contour of this piece by pausing slightly on the peaks (the high A in mm. 3 and 15, and the high C in m. 6).

Technique: Use rest stroke on the melody. Notice the dotted half note bass in mm. 3 and 15. This allows your first finger to play the F on the 1st string. Try setting your right-hand thumb on the 6th string at the rest on beat 4 to stop any noise caused by the transition. Similarly, set your right-hand fingers *ima* on the treble strings at mm. 8 and 16 to stop them from ringing as you play the last bass notes of these sections.

Try a 1st finger guide between mm. 4–5. In mm. 3 and 15, set your 2nd finger on the 1st string G before you lift your 4th finger off the A. At mm. 10 and 14, just lay your finger across the first string for the 1/3 bar

and then move back to the original position. Do not take the finger off the C; instead, just pivot back and forth.

Tárrega—*Lágrima* (p. 112)

Interpretation: The next two pieces by Tárrega should give you more freedom for expression than many in this volume. *Lágrima* literally means *teardrop* in Spanish and your interpretation should reflect this image. It is interesting that since the piece starts and ends in the major key instead of minor, the "teardrop" may well be one of sentiment rather than sadness.

The piece should maintain a lyrical, singing quality. In fact, it would be helpful to sing the melody to decide which natural inflections you would add. Allow yourself some freedom with the rhythm by using rubato.

The first measure can begin tentatively with a broken chord and then accelerate slightly toward the top of the phrase, backing off again as you go into the next measure. This idea should even be more pronounced in the minor section at m. 13. Rush toward the high D in the following measure, then pause on that note before you fall off into the run. Preceding that, in m. 12, make a slight break between beats two and three, where the two B's are played on different strings to highlight their different functions of accompaniment and melody.

The last repeat of the major section should be more reflective than the first two times through. For a dramatic effect, pause on the high A in m. 6 while stopping all the other strings from ringing. Add plenty of vibrato before falling off into the next measure. (Segovia would often use this technique to feature a lovely melody note.)

Technique: The bass lines in mm. 1, 3, 5, 6, and 13 can cause distracting squeaks if you do not lift your bass note finger straight up off the 4th string when shifting. In most of these measures you will still have the 4th finger on the 1st string as a guide finger for smoothness.

The fingering of m. 6 allows for a beautiful ascending harp-like sound by letting all the notes ring. I have chosen to use full bars instead of partial ones in mm. 7 and 9 for dampening purposes. Also dampen the low E in m. 11 with the back of the thumb as you play the 4th string A on the next beat. Be sure to have a silent transition in the following measure going from the bar VII to the first position. Play cleanly, eliminating any extraneous noise. The focus of this piece is not speed or dexterity. It is one of playing soulfully and legato with a beautiful sound, allowing your interpretation to transcend technical difficulties.

Tárrega–*Adelita* (p. 113)

Interpretation: This piece is similar to the last, and they are often performed as a pair. A lovely waltz, it begins and ends in the minor key with the parallel major key used for the middle section. The opening theme should have a sighing quality with a lot of rubato. The notes in m. 4 should overlap slightly and rush towards the repeat of the theme in the next measure.

You may wish rush the major section slightly. Pay attention to phrasing and the rise and fall of the melody. Notice the phrase in mm. 9 and 10 that is repeated an octave lower in m. 13. Be sure to bring this line out.

On the final repeat of the minor section in m. 7, you may wish to try this famous "Segovian" technique: roll the last chord, stop all strings but the melody, pause slightly with vibrato, and use a portamento to the next chord. It creates a very expressive ending to this beautiful little piece.

Technique: Plant your 1st finger on the first string (9th fret) along with your 3rd and 4th fingers before you pull-off in the first measure. This will give you a solid slur and aid in the transition to the B. Try rest stroke on the melody in the first section, except for m. 4.

The grace notes in mm. 11, 12, and 14 are the most difficult aspect of this piece. First practice the piece without the grace notes, learning the bar chord positions and the feel of the section. Practice the grace note chords separately. You might even desire to create

an exercise with them. Try playing the last beat of m. 11 (chord with grace notes and following C#) on the 9th fret, then on the 8th, then the 7th, etc. This will become harder as you descend, so playing it in context of the piece will be easier than what you have just practiced.

In m. 13, use more force on you right-hand index finger on the last chord to help bring out the melody on the 4th string.

Measure 14 contains a portamento where you play the G# after sliding to it. This phrase should be played with rubato, and be sure to watch the intonation. Play the portamento lightly so as to not hear every half-step in the slide.

Fortea–*Estudio* (p. 114)

Interpretation: There are two approaches to this piece. It can be used as a fast technical arpeggio study, or it can be a slow, beautiful flowing arpeggio. If the first option is selected, you will accent the bass note of every measure and think of the *sextuplet* (group of six notes) as one unit. If you play it slower, you can think of each sextuplet as a measure of ¾ with accents on the 1st, 3rd, and 5th notes, as an alternate interpretation.

The arpeggio has four separate voices, each played by a different finger. Add extra emphasis to any moving voice to highlight the motion.

Technique: Relax the right hand as much as possible. For extra speed, plant all fingers of the arpeggio on the strings as you play the first bass note of each pattern, Use *pimami* throughout for a consistent sound, even on the more difficult wider-spaced arpeggios. Your nails must be filed correctly for even sound and speed.

To facilitate left-hand changes, it is often more expedient to add the fingers as you need them rather than setting the whole chord down at once. Use guide fingers wherever possible, especially mm. 15–16 (A# to B), mm. 17–18 (D# to E), and mm. 33–34 (2nd and 4th fingers on shift). Pivot fingers are important in mm. 5–6 and 7–8 (1st and 4th fingers) and mm. 16–17 (2nd finger). The stretch at mm. 38 is difficult, so relax the hand as much as possible before the stretch. Pivot on the 3rd finger C, and add the other fingers as you come to them. For extra practice, try playing each sextuplet twice or four times.

Barrios–*Estudio del Ligado* (p. 116)

Interpretation: This virtuosic piece is basically an exercise in slurs. It should be played quite quickly to achieve a brilliant effect. You can start the first run slightly below speed and accelerate into the measure as you descend. A ritard is also effective at the end of

m. 4, before the first measure is repeated. The repeated slurs in mm. 10–16 build tension because of their static motion combined with the chromatic alterations in the bass line. This will provide opportunity for tone color and dynamic changes. It is a nice break between the very similar outer sections of the piece, where the only differences are between mm. 2 and 18 and between mm. 6 and 22.

Technique: Practice this piece with enough volume to build stamina for the left hand. Besides endurance, the primary difficulty lies in achieving evenness of sound and evenness of rhythm in each slurred triplet. Play directly on the left-hand fingertip, using enough force to sound the hammer-on and pull-off with a consistent volume. There will be a slight accent on the first of each triplet, but this should not be overdone. Avoid hammering-on or pulling-off too quickly to maintain an even triplet.

When descending the neck in the first measure, be sure to keep your 2nd finger on the string as a guide. At the end of m. 4, use your 1st finger as a guide from F# to G# and on into the next measure, where you will have both the 1st and 2nd fingers on the string. The 3rd finger is an important guide in m. 13, and I suggest keeping the 1st finger on the first string from m. 12 for extra support (planting it on the 2nd fret) until the shift.

For practice in obtaining speed and accuracy, play one triplet plus the very next note. When that is mastered, play two triplets plus one note. Keep adding to this pattern until you have completed a passage.

Romance–*Anonymous* (p. 117)

Interpretation: One of the most famous and beloved of all classical guitar pieces, this little Spanish folk song has appeared as everything from a movie theme to background music for Olympic skaters. The beautiful haunting melody should sing out above the rest of the arpeggio. Add vibrato to help sustain the melody. On chords, apply vibrato to the whole chord parallel to the neck. This will be especially effective in places like m. 10, where you can vibrato and pause slightly on the 1st or 2nd beat. Accent descending basses in m. 15 and in the parallel major section, m. 31. Also try starting the major section (m. 17) a little faster to accentuate the key change.

Technique: Use rest stroke on melody (first note of every triplet) in places where you desire added emphasis. The bars at mm. 9 and 21 are difficult to get to. Jump to the bar, then you may wish to pause slightly (musically) while you set the other fingers on the strings. For a smooth transition after these bars, try playing the open bass note in the next measure slightly before the melody note. This gives you some extra time to get the melody note ready.

The stretch at m. 27 is easier if you relax the left hand. If you wish, take your thumb off the back of the neck to give you more stretch. You can bar just two strings if that is easier, but the half-bar makes a smoother transition from the previous measure.

Use an all flesh strum on the last chord. Be sure to get enough high note in the chord.

Music is the shorthand of emotion. Emotions which let themselves be described in words with such difficulty, are directly conveyed to man in music, and in that is its power and significance.

–Leo Tolstoy

Maestro Andrés Segovia

ESTUDIO

See Notes, p. 107

Francisco Tárrega

LÁGRIMA

See Notes, p. 107

FRANCISCO TÁRREGA

ADELITA

See Notes, p. 108

FRANCISCO TÁRREGA

ESTUDIO

See Notes, p. 108

DANIEL FORTEA

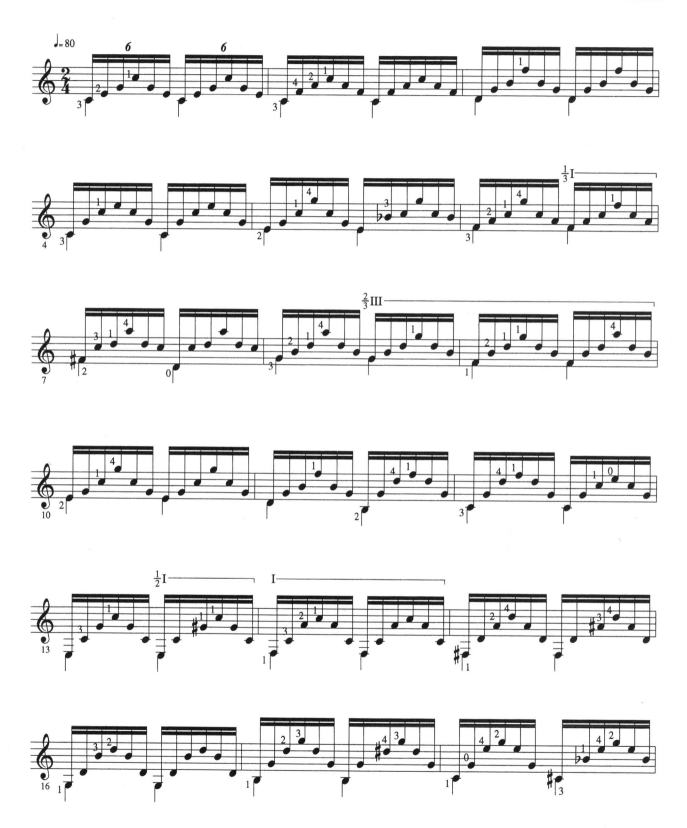

ESTUDIO DEL LIGADO

See Notes, p. 108

AGUSTÍN BARRIOS

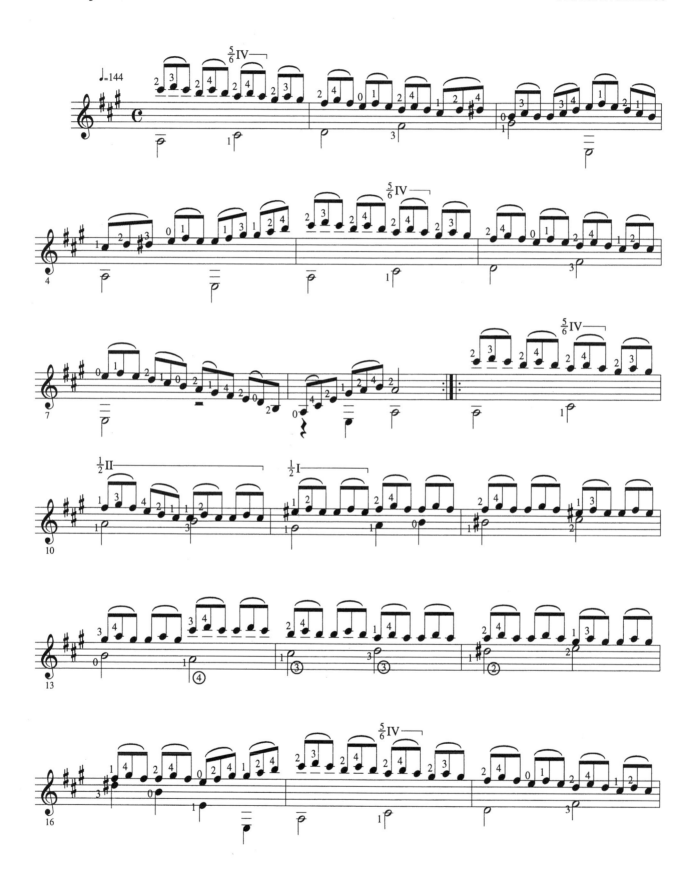

ROMANCE

See Notes, p. 109

ANONYMOUS

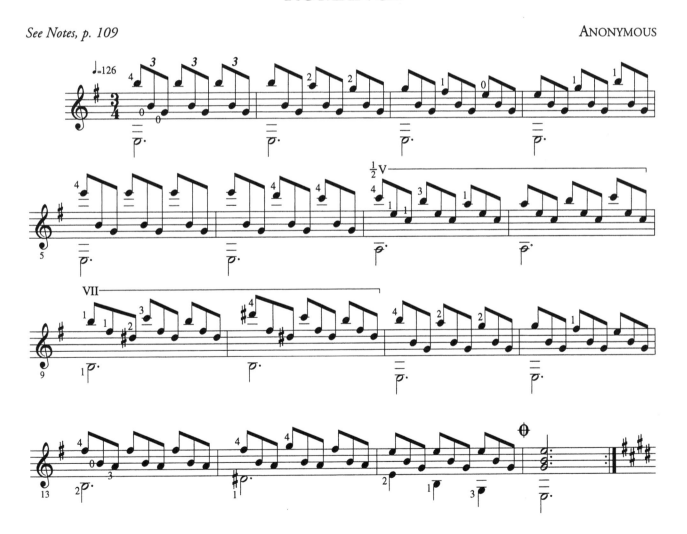

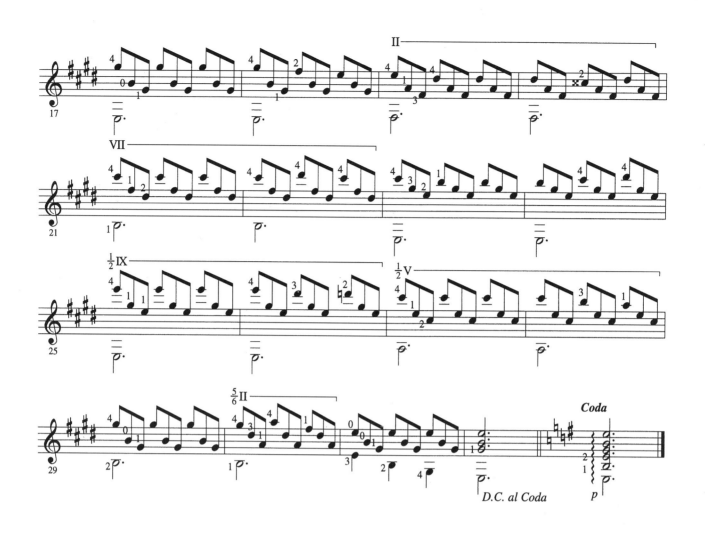

The beauty of the guitar resides in its soft and persuasive voice, and its poetry cannot be equaled by any other instrument.

—Andrés Segovia

Modern Period
(1910–present)

The Modern period has seen expanded chromaticism, dissonance, parallelism, complex rhythms, and unusual combinations of instruments in ensemble. Composers have taken instruments to their limits in every aspect. Some of these composers work within traditional musical forms and keys; others use free form, whole tone or other exotic scales, atonal harmonies, and a variety of textures, colors, and percussive effects. During our modern era many renowned composers of international stature dedicated music to Segovia, who single-handedly inspired and commissioned a modern repertoire for his beloved guitar. Many of these works adhere to traditional form, but they generally include expanded concepts in tonality and texture. Some modern music borrows liberally from American contemporary sources such as folk, jazz, or blues. Other composers use ethnic influences such as Spanish or Latin-American. Many of today's greatest composers are in the film industry, writing complex symphonic scores for television and motion pictures.

Notable Composers: Bartok, Bernstein, Copeland, Hindemith, MacDowell, Prokofiev, Rachmaninoff, Schönberg, Scriabin, Shostakovich, Stravinsky, Vaughan Williams. *For guitar:* Arnold, Bennett, Berkeley, Britten, Brouwer, Carlevaro, Castelnuovo-Tedesco, Dodgson, Duarte, Henze, Lauro, Martin, Mompou, Moreno-Torroba, Ohana, Ponce, Poulenc, Rak, Rodrigo, Roussel, Ruiz-Pipó, Sagreras, Tansman, Turina, Villa-Lobos, Walton, York.

Suggested Repertoire:

Brouwer, Leo
Ten Etudes

Carlevaro, Abel
Preludio Americano #3 (Campo)

Castelnuovo-Tedesco, Mario
Tarantella
Platero y Yo
Sonata
Concerto in D

Duarte, John
English Suite
Variations on a Catalan Folk Song

Lauro, Antonio
Venezuelan Waltzes
Suite Venezolano

Mompou, Federico
Suite Compastelana

Moreno-Torroba, Federico
Sonatina
Suite Castellana
Castles of Spain
Pieces Characteristiques

Ponce, Manuel
Six Preludes
Sonata III
Sonata Romantica

Ponce (cont.)
Sonatina Meridional
Suite in A Minor
Preludio (in the style of Weiss)
Concierto del Sur

Rodrigo, Joaquin
Fandango
En los Trigales
Sarabande Lointaine
Fantasia para un Gentilhombre
Concierto de Aranjuez

Tansman, Alexander
Danza Pomposa
Cavatina
Suite in Modo Polonico

Turina, Joaquin
Hommage a Tárrega
Fandanguillo
Ráfaga
Seviallanas

Villa-Lobos, Heitor
Five Preludes
Twelve Etudes
Suite Popular
Choros #1
Concerto

Walton, William
Five Bagatelles

Three Duets

The following three duets are performance scores from my *Virtuoso Duets* recording with David Brandon. They appear here exactly as we recorded them. For additional interpretive ideas not marked in the music, refer to the recording.

LA ROSSIGNOL

ANONYMOUS

DREWRIES ACCORDES

ANONYMOUS

CANON

GEORG PHILIPP TELEMANN

127

Appendix A

Sound Production

Nail Filing

John Williams once told me that you can never learn anything by looking at another guitarist's nails, and I think perhaps he is right. There are, however, some guidelines which I would like to pass along regarding how I personally file my fingernails. It is important in the broadest sense to file your nails so that you can do two things: 1) produce a wide variety of tonal colors and 2) traverse the string as quickly and easily as possible.

As a general rule, it is important for me to file the nails of all the fingers (*pima*) so that they cross the string with the same amount of effort (or resistance to the string). I have found there is no perfect shape for my nails. They seem to play well in a variety of shapes and lengths. Far more important is the interaction or relationship of the nails to each other. Thus, the length and shape of one nail can affect another. This interdependence may be further complicated by the wearing down of nails caused by performance or heavy practice.

The length of nails for most players varies from barely visible over the fingertip to ⅛" long. Generally speaking, the shorter the nail, the faster you can play (but accompanied with it is a "pad-like" thuddy tone). Longer nails (depending on your stroke) can produce perhaps a more beautiful tone but may possibly slow your ability to play rapidly. Also, when the nail gets too long, the sound becomes somewhat tinny and brittle and also produces extraneous clicks which you want to avoid. In general, though, I would rather my nails be a touch too long than too short. Nails can feel shorter in concert due to the warm temperature created by intense stage lighting (which causes your fingers to swell). Fingernails can also wear down with hard practice.

When I am filing my nails in preparation for a full concert program, I file them (with guitar in hand) in response to the most difficult runs, arpeggios, or other challenging sections of pieces on the program. I strive to achieve a workable compromise between all the difficult areas. (I do not suggest, however, reshaping your nails on the day of a performance nor experimenting with a different nail shape too close to a concert day.)

To file my nails I most often use an Alpha–9™ nail file which has a variety of surfaces. Diamond Deb™ and Revlon™ files are also good, provided that you temper the coarseness of a new file. The nail shape is determined mainly by how far the nail should ride on the string from its point of contact to the point of release. These are arbitrary points, however, and will change depending on the type of stroke involved. Some guitarists feel that a momentary catch in the corner of the nail followed by a quick release is most desirable for speed, and I agree. When I began to play the guitar at age eleven, I filed my nails based on how I felt they should look. I now file them more according to feel and sound. I usually take off less nail rather than more, making small corrections as needed. In fact, my nails usually feel better after they have been worn in slightly by playing.

After I achieve the basic nail shape, I must polish the edge of the nail with finishing paper to avoid a raspy sound. To create this smooth nail edge, I use 3M #500 Tri-M-ite™ Fre-Cut (open coat) sandpaper. It is important to polish the nail in a manner which preserves the thickness of the nail and avoids a knife-like edge. (fig. 21)

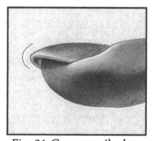 

Fig. 21 Correct nail edge.   Incorrect knife-like edge.

The finishing paper is also good for making slight modifications and can shorten a nail without significantly altering the "worn in" shape. I will also frequently make very small corrections using one of the bass strings as a file against the section of the nail that needs modification. Sometimes I will "play" the fingernail against the paper as it is folded over the file or part of the guitar for the same purpose.

Another principle is for me to have a flat surface to the nail edge. That is, the nail should be able to sit evenly on the plane of the nail file without uneven ridges and no hook shape to the nail. (fig. 22)

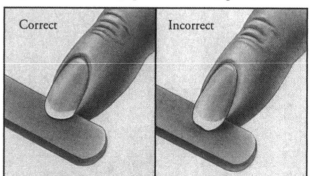

Fig. 22 The nail should sit evenly on the file.

Because my nails are very arched in shape, I file them slightly biased to the left-hand side in order to reduce some of the natural curve. This reduces the riding time on the string. Guitarists with hooked nails will need to file more off in the curved areas to help create a flat edge.

I use nail enamel on the *p, i, m,* and *a* fingers (generally three coats) to protect them from wear, especially from rasgueados. However, it is essential to remove any enamel from the final 1/16" of the nail edge with nail polish remover so it does not affect the sound.

When a nail splits or cracks, nail glue (Super Glue™) may be used for a quick repair. However, I have found more strength with the combination of nail glue and a double *silk wrap* over the entire top of the nail followed by a coat of enamel (such as Hard-As-Nails™). I find that it does not hurt the sound, nor is it a problem in nail growth or filing. It is also cosmetically unnoticeable. Acrylic nails or Player's Nails™ can be used when the entire nail has broken off.

I keep the length of the little finger fairly short, just long enough to play a rasgueado with a good sound. Left-hand nails should be kept short yet long enough to stabilize the pad of the fingertip (on slurs, trills, etc.). When they are cut too short, there is too much "wobble" in the fingertip. Of course, when they are too long they interfere not only with the position of the left hand playing on the fingertips but also with slurs and trills, etc.

Ultimately I feel it is necessary for each individual guitarist to experiment with a variety of nail shapes and lengths that best suit his or her playing style. Never give up, but with determination, strive for a balance between speed and a beautiful sound. There is not a cut and dried mold for the perfect nail shape—because every person's hand and nail shapes are different. I have noticed through the years, though, that the thicker the nail, the rounder and warmer the sound; and the thinner the nail, the thinner, brighter, and more metallic the sound. Thus, you must take advantage of all the thickness of nail you have. It is very easy to get a thin sound on the guitar but very difficult to get a warm, rich, beautiful sound. It is that quality of sound achieved by Segovia on the guitar which has been my example through the years.

Tone Production

To create a beautiful sound on the guitar, you must learn to properly activate the string. First, set your right hand just behind the soundhole in a regular playing position. (fig. 23) For a normal, clear tone you should use a combination of nail and flesh. (fig. 24) The stroke should begin on the side of the fingernail (point of contact) and should ride toward the center (point of release). (fig. 25)

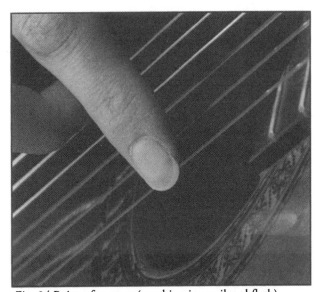

Fig. 24 Point of contact (combination nail and flesh).

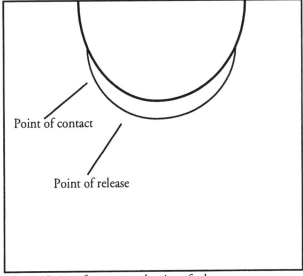

Point of contact

Point of release

Fig. 25 Point of contact and point of release.

129

Whether you play off the left or right side of the fingernail, the point of contact is where the fingertip, fingernail, and string meet simultaneously before activating the string. (fig. 26) The glide toward the point of release should be fairly short and quick. I suggest learning first to play off the left side of the nail. At this stage rest stroke will be easier to execute than free stroke, but both should be practiced.

There are two common errors with placement which will produce an unwanted click or buzz: 1) starting too far back on the flesh and bouncing to the nail, or 2) starting too far forward on the nail while the string is vibrating. In a properly executed stroke, the pad of the fingertip will touch the string just slightly before the nail does (to dampen the string). In an instant, when you press slightly to make the stroke, you will find yourself at the proper point of contact ready to activate the string.

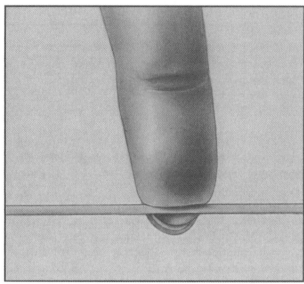

Fig. 26 Point of Contact (combination nail and flesh).

A stroke with the thumbnail will generally be made with the thumb at roughly a 45° angle from the string. The stroke should begin near the center of the nail and should ride toward the left side of the nail to release. (fig. 27) For an extremely full, dolce thumb sound (reminiscent of Segovia), try "slicing" the string from the left side of the thumbnail riding toward the center. (fig. 28) For additional tonal variation, you can play all flesh or use the side of the thumb with a slight bit of nail to create a raspy effect.

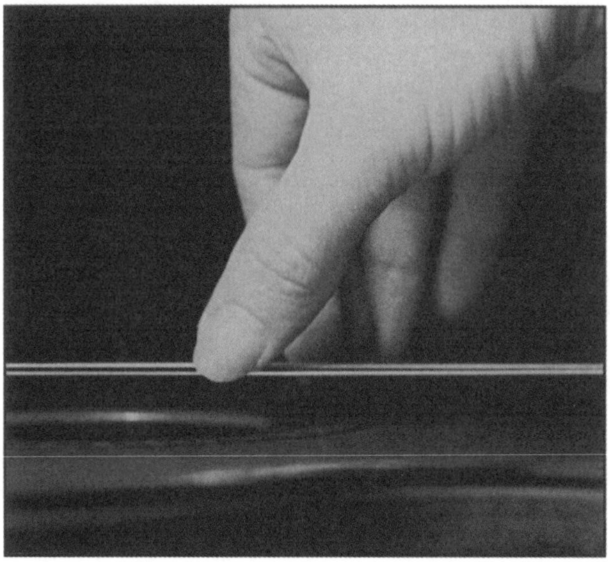

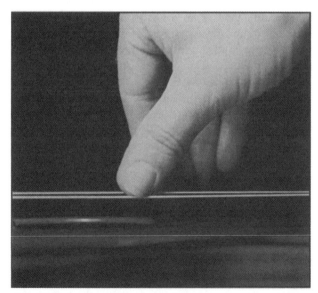

Fig. 27 Normal thumb stroke position.

Fig. 28 Dolce thumb stroke position.

Once you have achieved a basic sound, you can experiment with dolce and ponticello positions. The following chart explains four distinct methods of creating both dolce and ponticello sounds. You can use one or all of these techniques to create a wide variety of tonal colors.

Dolce (fig. 29)

1) Play over the sound hole.

2) Combine left side of nail with flesh.

3) Direct the stroke toward the left shoulder such that the strings vibrate parallel to the face of the guitar (sometimes termed a "slicing" stroke).

4) Finger the left hand in upper positions.

In addition, I have found that relaxing the first joint of the fingers and using more of a bent wrist produces a warm mellow sound. Note: When playing in the extreme upper positions on the guitar, you will need to play in more of a dolce position to help equalize the sound of the shorter string length.

Ponticello (fig. 30)

1) Play near the bridge.

2) Use mostly nail (center of nail).

3) Pluck outward such that the strings vibrate perpendicularly to the face of the guitar.

4) Finger the left hand in lower positions (closer to the first position).

I also play with stiffer fingers and a straighter wrist, sometimes pivoting from the elbow while resting more on the middle of the forearm. This is most often done free stroke.

Fig. 29 Dolce position.

Fig. 30 Ponticello position.

Developing a beautiful sound with a diversity of tonal colors can be one of the most challenging and yet rewarding aspects of playing the guitar. Experiment with the different methods of tone production and strive to develop your own unique sound to facilitate maximum musical expression.

Appendix B

The following is a list of recordings of the pieces that appear in the repertoire section of this book. Again, I believe it is valuable to listen to various interpretations—not to copy a particular one, but to expand your thinking in order to develop your own individual style. It is especially important to listen to works performed on their original instruments when studying transcriptions. For example, listen to Bach's *Prelude* from the *1st Cello Suite* performed on cello and Scarlatti's *Sonata in A* performed on harpsichord.

Repertoire Discography
Compiled by John Nelson

COMPOSER	TITLE	ARTIST	RECORDING
Renaissance			
ANONYMOUS	*Danza & Gagliarda*	Andrés Segovia	THE ART OF ANDRÉS SEGOVIA DECCA DL 9795
	Canzone	Andrés Segovia	SEGOVIA-GUITAR SOLOS DECCA DL 8022
ANONYMOUS	*Salterello*	Christopher Parkening	THE ARTISTRY OF CHRISTOPHER PARKENING EMI CLASSICS CDC 7 54853
		Andrés Segovia	SEGOVIA-GUITAR SOLOS DECCA DL 8022
L. MILAN	*Pavane #1 in C*	Andrés Segovia	THE SEGOVIA COLLECTION, VOL. 5 MCA CLASSICS MCAD-42071
		Julian Bream	MUSIC OF SPAIN: LUTE, VOL. 1 RCA ARL1-3435
R. JOHNSON	*Alman*	José Tomás	GUITAR RECITAL CROWN SW-2001
J.B. BESARD	*Branle & Volte*	Liona Boyd	LIONA BOOT MASTER CONCERT SERIES BMC-3006
		Julian Bream	LUTE MUSIC FROM THE ROYAL COURTS OF EUROPE RCA VICTOR LSC-2924
J. DOWLAND	*Galliard*	Christopher Parkening	PLEASURES OF THEIR COMPANY ANGEL CDC-7 47196 2
		Andrés Segovia	SEGOVIA AND THE GUITAR DECCA DL 79931
J. DOWLAND	*Allemande*	Christopher Parkening	PLEASURES OF THEIR COMPANY ANGEL CDC-7 47196 2
FOR FURTHER LISTENING		Paul O'Dette	
Baroque			
R. DE VISÉE	*Prelude & Bourrée* *(Suite in D minor)*	Andrés Segovia	AN ANDRÉS SEGOVIA CONCERT DECCA DL 9638
		Julian Bream	BAROQUE GUITAR RCA VICTOR 60494-2-RV
G. SANZ	*Pavanas*	Julian Bream	BAROQUE GUITAR RCA VICTOR 60494-2-RV
		Celedonio Romero	SPANISH GUITAR MUSIC CONTEMPORARY S 8502
J.S. BACH	*Bourrée in E minor* *(Lute Suite No. 1)*	John Williams	BACH: THE FOUR LUTE SUITES CBS MK 42204
		Andrés Segovia	THE SEGOVIA COLLECTION, VOL.4 MCA CLASSICS MCAD-42070
	Prelude *(Cello Suite No. 1)*	Andrés Segovia	THE SEGOVIA COLLECTION, VOL. 4 MCA CLASSICS MCAD-420
		Christopher Parkening	THE ARTISTRY OF CHRISTOPHER PARKENING EMI CLASSICS CDC 7 54853 2 5
		John Williams	THE CLASSIC GUITAR SINE QUA NON 101
D. SCARLATTI	*Sonata in A (L. 483)*	Andrés Segovia	THE SEGOVIA COLLECTION, VOL. 4 MCA CLASSICS MCAD-42070
		Carlos Barbosa-Lima	A SCARLATTI GUITAR RECITAL ABC AUDIO TREASURY ABC/ATS-20005
		Oscar Ghiglia	PLAYS SCARLATTI AND OTHER BAROQUE MASTERS ANGEL S-37015

D. SCARLATTI	*Sonata in A (L. 483)*	Angel Romero	**CLASSICAL VIRTUOSO** ANGEL S-36093
		Eliot Fisk	**PERFORMS MUSIC BY BAROQUE COMPOSERS** MUSICMASTERS MDD 20090K
FOR FURTHER LISTENING		Pablo Casals Wanda Landowska	

Classical

M. CARCASSI	*Study in E minor (Op.60, No.19)*	David Tanenbaum	**ESTUDIOS** GSP 1000CD
		Christopher Parkening	**ROMANZA** ANGEL SFO-36021
	Study in A (Op. 60, No. 3)	David Tanenbaum	**ESTUDIOS** GSP 1000CD
		Alexandre Lagoya	**BOCCHERINI/PAGANINI/SCARLATTI/ CARCASSI** RCA VICTOR LSC-3142
	Study in A minor (Op.60, No.7)	David Tanenbaum	**ESTUDIOS** GSP 1000CD
		John Mills	**MUSIC FROM THE STUDENT REP., SERIES 2** GUITAR G102
F. SOR	*Study in A (Op. 6, No. 2)*	Andrés Segovia	**THE SEGOVIA COLLECTION, VOL. 7** MCA CLASSICS MCAD-42073
		Christopher Parkening	**THE ARTISTRY OF CHRISTOPHER PARKENING** EMI CLASSICS CDC 7 54853 2 5
		John Williams	**SOR: TWENTY STUDIES FOR GUITAR** WESTMINSTER GOLD WGS-8137
		David Tanenbaum	**ESTUDIOS** GSP 1000CD
	Study in B minor (Op. 35, No. 22)	Andrés Segovia	**THE SEGOVIA COLLECTION, VOL. 3** MCA CLASSICS MCAD-42069
		John Williams	**SOR: TWENTY STUDIES FOR GUITAR** WESTMINSTER GOLD WGS-8137
		Manuel Barrueco	**THE ROMANTIC GUITAR** MENUET 160001-2
		David Tanenbaum	**ESTUDIOS** GSP 1000CD
	Minuet in C (Op. 25)	Julian Bream	**BAROQUE GUITAR** RCA VICTOR 60494-2-RV
	Waltz in E (Op. 32, No. 2)	Andrés Segovia	**THE SEGOVIA COLLECTION, VOL. 7** MCA CLASSICS MCAD-42073
		Oscar Ghiglia	**RODRIGO/SOR/PONCE** RICERCARE ERC 1718
M. GIULIANI	General listening	David Starobin	**MAURO GIULIANI: SOLO GUITAR MUSIC** BCD 9029

Romantic

F. TÁRREGA	*Estudio*	Liona Boyd	**MINIATURES FOR GUITAR** BOOT RECORDS BOS-7181
	Lágrima	Julian Bream	**IMPRESSIONS FOR GUITAR** RCA XRL-17181
		Liona Boyd	**MINIATURES FOR GUITAR** BOOT RECORDS BOS-7181
	Adelita	Andrés Segovia	**MASTERS OF THE GUITAR** DECCA DL 9794
		Pepe Romero	**WORKS FOR GUITAR: ALBÉNIZ, TÁRREGA** PHILLIPS 416 384-2
		Angel Romero	**SPANISH VIRTUOSO** ANGEL S-36094
D. FORTEA	*Estudio*	- - - - -	- - - - -
A. BARRIOS	General Listening	John Williams	**PLAYS MUSIC OF AGUSTÍN BARRIOS MANGORÉ** COLUMBIA M 35 145
		Agustín Barrios	**THE COMPLETE HISTORICAL RECORDINGS** CHANTERELLE CHR 002
ANONYMOUS	*Romance*	Christopher Parkening	**PARKENING-THE GREAT RECORDINGS** EMI CLASSICS ZDCB 54905 2 7
		Pepe Romero	**FAMOUS SPANISH GUITAR MUSIC** PHILLIPS 411 033-2
		Manuel Barrueco	**THE ROMANTIC GUITAR** MENUET 160001-2

Fingerboard Chart

A Personal Note From Christopher Parkening...

I have a commitment to personal excellence which at its heart seeks to honor and glorify the Lord with my life and the music that I play. People often ask how my faith affects my music and my career as a concert guitarist. As a Christian, I find it helpful to contemplate verses from the Bible before and even during a performance. One of my favorites is PHILIPPIANS 4:6–7: *"Be anxious for nothing; but in everything by prayer and supplication with thanksgiving let your requests be made known unto God. And the peace of God, which passeth all understanding, shall keep your hearts and minds through Christ Jesus."* It is interesting to note that it does not say God will answer every request in the way you would expect. It does say that by trusting in Him with thanksgiving, you will have the peace to handle whatever circumstance or situation that occurs. In other words, you place the burden of responsibility upon the Lord, trusting that His will would be done. That is what gives you the peace.

Here are some other helpful verses:

ROMANS 8:28 *And we know that all things work together for good to them that love God, to them who are the called according to his purpose.*

PHILIPPIANS 4:8–9 *Finally, brethren, whatsoever things are true, whatsoever things are honest, whatsoever things are just, whatsoever things are pure, whatsoever things are lovely, whatsoever things are of good report; if there be any virtue, and if there be any praise, think on these things. Those things, which ye have both learned, and received, and heard, and seen in me, do: and the God of peace shall be with you.*

II CORINTHIANS 12:9 *And he said unto me, My grace is sufficient for thee: for my strength is made perfect in weakness. Most gladly therefore will I rather glory in my infirmities, that the power of Christ may rest upon me.*

ISAIAH 26:3 *Thou wilt keep him in perfect peace, whose mind is stayed on thee: because he trusteth in thee.*

PROVERBS 3:5–6 *Trust in the LORD with all thine heart; and lean not unto thine own understanding. In all thy ways acknowledge him, and he shall direct thy paths.*

I PETER 5:5b–7 *...be clothed with humility: for God resisteth the proud, and giveth grace to the humble. Humble yourselves therefore under the mighty hand of God, that he may exalt you in due time: casting all your care upon him; for he careth for you.*

ISAIAH 12:2 *Behold, God is my salvation: I will trust, and not be afraid.*

JOHN 3:16 *For God so loved the world, that he gave his only begotten Son, that whosoever believeth in him should not perish, but have everlasting life.*

Most people believe you need to be confident in order to play a good concert. I understand, however, that God does not want us to take confidence in our own ability, and I realize that I am inadequate for the task ahead. This requires me to depend totally on God's power and grace to sustain me. Likewise then, it is a source of peace and comfort to look back and remember God's grace in past performances and trust that His grace will be sufficient for this one as well. Backstage, I constantly remind myself of what I know to be true. For example, *"All things work together for good..."*

Personally, I ultimately desire to please the Lord with my music. I dedicate every performance to my Lord and Savior Jesus Christ and consequently, the "approval" of the audience is secondary. For more insight on this topic, I recommend reading *Anxiety Attacked* by John MacArthur, Jr. (Victor Books).

Many people have asked me how to become an excellent guitarist. I answer, "Be a hard-working perfectionist," which personally makes up for my lack of talent in a lot of areas. Our goal should be to overcome what we lack in talent or ability by what we have in dedication and commitment. This takes self-discipline—the ability to regulate your conduct by principles and sound judgment, rather than by impulse, desire, high pressure, or social custom. It is the ability to subordinate the body to what is right and what is best. Self-discipline means nothing more than to order the priorities of your life. It is the bridge between thought and accomplishment, the glue that binds inspiration to achievement. For me, as a Christian, self-discipline is first of all to obey the word of God—the Bible. It is to bring my desires, my emotions, my feelings, and all that is in my life under the control of God supremely, so that I may live an obedient life which has as its goal the glory of God.

The aim and final reason of all music should be none else but the glory of God.

—Johann Sebastian Bach

About The Authors...

CHRISTOPHER PARKENING ranks as one of the world's preeminent virtuosos of the classical guitar. His concerts and recordings consistently receive the highest worldwide acclaim. *The Washington Post* cited "his stature as the leading guitar virtuoso of our day, combining profound musical insight with complete technical mastery of his instrument." Parkening is the recognized heir to the legacy of the great Spanish guitarist Andrés Segovia, who proclaimed that "Christopher Parkening is a great artist — he is one of the most brilliant guitarists in the world."

Parkening's rare combination of dramatic virtuosity and eloquent musicianship has captivated audiences from New York to Tokyo. He has performed at the White House, appeared with Placido Domingo on *Live from Lincoln Center,* participated in Carnegie Hall's 100th Anniversary celebration, and performed twice on the internationally televised Grammy® Awards.

Parkening has appeared on many nationally broadcast television programs including *The Tonight Show, Good Morning America, 20/20, CBS Sunday Morning,* and *The Today Show.* Having been voted "Best Classical Guitarist" in a nationwide reader's poll of *Guitar Player* magazine for many years running, he was placed in their *Gallery of the Greats* along with Andrés Segovia, John Williams, and Julian Bream.

Parkening has amassed a prolific discography on Angel records and EMI Classics. He is the recipient of two Grammy® nominations in the category of Best Classical Recording for *Parkening and the Guitar* and *The Pleasures of Their Company* (a collaboration with soprano Kathleen Battle). In celebration of Parkening's 25th year as a best-selling EMI artist, a collection of his most popular recordings entitled *Christopher Parkening – The Great Recordings* was released. EMI also released his critically acclaimed recording of Joaquín Rodrigo's *Concierto de Aranjuez* and *Fantasia para un gentilhombre,* together with the world premiere of William Walton's *Five Bagatelles for Guitar and Orchestra.* Rodrigo himself was present for the recording, which he called "magnificent."

Other important recording releases include *A Tribute to Segovia* (dedicated to the great Spanish guitarist and recorded on one of the Maestro's own concert guitars) and *Parkening Plays Vivaldi* with the Academy of St. Martin in the Fields featuring favorite concertos plus the world premiere recording of Peter Warlock's *Capriol (Suite for Guitar and String Orchestra).* Parkening also collaborated with Julie Andrews in *The Sounds of Christmas* with the London Symphony Orchestra on the Hallmark label, which sold over a million copies in its first year of release. Sony Classical also released his Christmas album with Kathleen Battle entitled *Angel's Glory.*

Parkening's commitment to his instrument extends beyond his demanding performance and recording schedule. Each summer, he teaches a series of master classes at Montana State University in Bozeman, Montana. He has authored *The Christopher Parkening Guitar Method, Volume I* (the companion to this volume), as well as numerous folios of guitar transcriptions and arrangements which he has recorded, all published by Hal Leonard Corporation.

Parkening has received commendations throughout his career honoring his dedication and artistry, including an honorary Doctorate of Music from Montana State University and the Outstanding Alumnus Award from the University of Southern California "in recognition of his outstanding international achievement and in tribute to his stature throughout the world as America's preeminent virtuoso of the classical guitar."

Christopher and his wife Theresa reside in Southern California. He is a world class fly-fishing and casting champion who has won the International Gold Cup Tarpon Tournament (the Wimbledon of fly-fishing) held in Islamorada, Florida.

DAVID BRANDON has made numerous concert and television appearances throughout North America, Europe, and Asia. The *Los Angeles Times* has called him "an outstanding technician whose precise control of details is stunning to experience." He has toured extensively with Christopher Parkening and performed with him on *Virtuoso Duets,* released by Angel/EMI. Brandon also appeared with Parkening on the Julie Andrews Hallmark Christmas album.

Brandon began playing guitar at age eight with instruction from his father. At thirteen, he attended master classes under Michael Lorimer as the youngest member of the class. After a year of study and performances in Spain and England, Brandon returned to the United States to study with Christopher Parkening on scholarship at Montana State University. He later studied with Andrés Segovia at the University of Southern California in his 1981 Master Class.

Brandon regularly gives master classes and lectures at colleges and universities across the nation. He has been the guitar advisor for the National Federation of Music Clubs and a judge for the Music Teachers National Association. David lives with his wife Sharee' and two sons in Lubbock, Texas, where he operates a private guitar studio.